# Living a Positive Life

A collection of stories by truly inspiring souls

# Living a Positive Life

A collection of stories by truly inspiring souls

Serenity Press Publishing

Copyright © 2014 Serenity Press Publishing.

All rights reserved. No part of this book may be used or reproduced by any means, graphic, electronic, or mechanical, including photocopying, recording, taping or by any information storage retrieval system without the written permission of the publisher except in the case of brief quotations embodied in critical articles and reviews.

All of the stories shared are personal journeys through life and are the responsibility of each author. Serenity Press Publishing does not take responsibility for any offense taken by the publishing of these stories and trusts that the author has received relevant permissions to publish them.

Serenity Press Publishing books may be ordered through booksellers or by contacting:

Serenity Press Publishing
www.serenitypress.org
serenitypress@hotmail.com

Because of the dynamic nature of the Internet, any web addresses or links contained in this book may have changed since publication and may no longer be valid. The views expressed in this work are solely those of the author and do not necessarily reflect the views of the publisher and the publisher hereby disclaims any responsibility for them.

The authors in this book do not dispense medical advice or prescribe the use of any technique as a form of treatment for physical, emotional, or medical problems without the advice of a physician, either directly or indirectly. The intent of the authors is only to offer information of a general nature to help you in your quest for emotional and spiritual well-being. In the event you use any of the information in this book for yourself, which is your constitutional right, the author and the publisher assume no responsibility for your actions.

ISBN: 978-0-9925231-9-0 (sc)
ISBN: 978-0-9923940-8-0 (e)

Printed in Australia

# Table of Contents

FROM MESS TO MENTOR
**JODIE FREEMAN** ............................................ 1

THE HEALING THAT COMES AFTER DEATH
**KYLIE YOUNG** ........................................26

THROUGH MY EYES
**CLAIRE HOWARD** ........................................46

SOUL SISTA JESS
**JESS WELSH** ........................................95

EMBRACING THE DREAM
**KAREN MC DERMOTT** .................................... 145

**BONUS** "ALL IT TAKES IS AN HOUR" ..............................
**ROD WILLNER** .................................... 153

# From Mess To Mentor

*Written by Jodie Freeman*

Never in my wildest dreams could I have imagined being where I am today. When I look back at my past, it almost seems like a bad dream, a nightmare in fact, one I didn't think I was ever going to wake up from. What changed? What brought me from the depths of despair to sheer happiness and joy? *I changed how I looked at life.* It sounds simple enough, but in reality it was far from that. It was one of the hardest things I've ever had to do. It's something I still have to work on every single day, but boy, is it worth it!

Let's take a step back to the beginning, right back into childhood, where most deep-seated issues seem to begin… with my parents.

My mother is a hard woman now, but she was even harder still back then. Her own mother passed away when she was a teenager, leaving her to look after a farm, a home, three other brothers and a sister, and her father who didn't mind a drink. She was born and raised out west, in the red dirt country, where you worked damn hard and you didn't complain about it. She missed out on the basics of genuine love and affection, and she carried on this pattern when my brother and I were born.

Mum "raised us to survive" as she puts it. She didn't raise us to be caring, compassionate members of a family. Because she herself had no other choice but to simply survive in her own teenage years, she wanted us to at least have those basic survival skills in case anything ever happened to her. Teaching us those skills was a good thing in itself, but when it's given *instead* of affection, rather than *as well as* affection, it's not all that great. This left a gaping hole in both my own, and I assume my brother's hearts. There wasn't that loving, gentle mother figure in our lives, just one that gave us the necessities that we needed to survive, and not much else. Her nickname was the "crowbar" or "ironing board" because whenever anyone tried to give her a hug, she became as stiff and cold as one.

I was not an easy baby to raise from my understanding. Apparently I cried and cried and simply wouldn't sleep, for no reason that any doctors could figure out, what they'd call colic these days. This would be a lot of strain on any person, and I can see how this would be difficult to deal with. My mum, dad and aunty all took it in turns to try to get me to sleep, and to get some sleep themselves. The only way I would sleep was if they took me for a drive in the car so, needless to say, they spent quite a bit of money on petrol at the time!

As a child growing up, I was labelled "different", "weird", or as my kindergarten teacher said, "there's something not quite right with that girl." I would say or do things that didn't fit into society's perception of being normal; therefore I was seen as being broken.

As a baby and toddler, I didn't like to be held or cuddled by mum, or by anyone else for that matter. Eventually mum got tired of trying and being pushed away, rejected in her eyes, so she just stopped trying. This led to me feeling abandoned and unloved as I got older. I didn't know until I was an adult that this was the behaviour I'd had as a baby; all I knew was that mum never gave me cuddles and I didn't know why. I assumed there must have been something wrong with me for her to not give me cuddles and show me affection. I took this personally and I took this to heart. My mum didn't know how to deal with having a child as "different" as I was, so I guess I felt like I was never accepted for just being me, that I was a failure as a person before I even grew up.

From what I remember as a young child, my dad was always my hero. I loved spending time with him on the farms we grew up on, watching him work on the farm machinery, listening to his stories about the crops and animals that he raised. I used to enjoy cuddles with dad at that stage, as well as spending time together. That all came to a stop though when the pastor of our church at the time thought it was a good idea on a men's camp to advise fathers not to get too close to their daughters, for fear of being accused of molesting them! Things were never the same after that, much to my dismay, and I could never understand what I'd done wrong to make him stop giving me the love and affection that he had been giving previously. First mum, now dad! I would ask myself, "What have I done?", "Am I a bad person?" and "What's wrong with me?" All of these things got compounded until I had it set in my mind that I was the cause of the problem. There must be something wrong with *me* for them both to stop showing me affection, and for mum to criticise and ridicule me the way she did.

Unbeknownst to anyone at the time, I suffered with Asperger's Syndrome, a milder form of Autism. I wasn't diagnosed with this until my early 30's, so this explained a lot of my queer behaviour that no one seemed to understand when I was younger, especially the fact that I didn't like to be touched. There are so many sensitivities that a person with Asperger's cannot handle; mine ranged from light, touch, smells, textures of food and sounds, just to name a few. Clumsiness was also a trait of mine that didn't help the situation. I would, almost every day, spill drinks, trip over my own feet or bang my knees and elbows on random things.

I also found it hard to remember things in the short term, such as homework or to bring my jumper home from school if I took it off. All of these things would irritate my mum to the point where she would snap at me every time, and it felt as if I was walking on a tightrope, never quite sure when I was going to fall and have a crash landing. There was never such thing as "an accident" at home, never a kind or understanding tone, never a "don't worry, we can clean that spill up." She would often call me names and put me down; her favourites were stupid, moron and idiot. She would make me feel so insignificant, worthless and plain dumb. She called me these names so often that eventually I began to believe it.

I'll never forget one day when I was helping her cook. I think I was around fourteen years old, and was helping her make macaroni and cheese... should be simple enough right? I should have put the casserole dish in the microwave, but I'd put it on the hot plate instead, and it wasn't a dish that could be put on the stove, so it cracked right down the middle. I heard the crack, realised what had happened, my heart skipped a beat and I looked over at mum, *cringing,* just waiting for the explosion. Waiting for her to lose her shit and yell at me and tell me what a stupid bloody idiot I was, "What were you thinking!", "Why would you do that, you bloody moron?!" but these insults never came. For once in my life, she didn't ridicule me for making what was a simple mistake; instead *she laughed!* This reaction was so out of the norm for her that I didn't know what to do. She couldn't comprehend that I was so conditioned to her reaction of calling me names that I simply expected it by this stage. It took me weeks to finally come to terms with the fact that there wasn't going to be any nasty repercussions for making that mistake, and that she really was OK with it.

Even to this day, I can recall that tension, that nervousness, waiting for the name calling. No matter how many times mum cursed me out; all I ever wanted was her love. Even to this day, it's a rare occasion when I get a hug from her; it's like pulling teeth really. Christmas and special occasions are usually the only times, and even then, it's usually under protest.

Being such a different kid, I had a lot of trouble at school with being teased. I changed schools a number of times when I was younger, for the fact that it was so horrible for me to go there every day. The Asperger's really made it hard for me to make or to *keep* friends. I was so quiet and shy that I often sat by myself and didn't play with or talk to anyone, or would hang out in the library. Asperger's often finds you not having very good social skills, and I definitely suffered with this issue a great deal. I often didn't know how to react in certain situations, and put my foot in it quite a bit, or would make inappropriate comments that others found strange or "out there".

I think back now, and realise just how much the other girls shut me out and made fun of me, more than I ever realised at the time, and of that I'm probably glad. I really relate to Sheldon from the TV show "The Big Bang Theory" in the way they often make fun of him straight to his face, but it goes right over his head, as he doesn't comprehend social etiquette or sarcasm.

We moved to the coast towards the end of year 8 for me, to give my brother and me some time to settle in before a new year began. I found this high school very frightening, as the number of people there was enormous compared to what I was used to, and my Asperger's went off the Richter scale. I was bullied here quite badly, and ended up having to speak to the school councillor, and began to suffer from depression because of this and everything else going on at home. The councillor spoke to the girls involved, and eventually it got better after it became worse for a while, but by this stage I was already quite depressed.

One day after school, I was avoiding being at home as usual and decided to go for a walk to the corner shop, just a block away for an ice cream. As I was on my way there I was approached by an older man in his forties who grabbed me and pulled me behind some bushes, with his hand over my mouth so that I wouldn't scream and was threatening me with what he'd do to me if I made a noise. My innocence was taken away from me that day; it felt as though the last piece of me that was sacred was stolen, just five weeks before my "sweet sixteen". Because I felt no support from my parents at the best of times, this was not something that I felt I could talk about with them, so I didn't. I didn't have friends I could tell either, so I kept it to myself. This was the last piece of light within me that had been extinguished, so I now sat in complete darkness all the time. I had been fractured before, but this broke me completely. I had already felt worthless, so this just compounded that feeling a hundred fold. I felt no care for myself anymore; all I felt was hate, anger and sadness.

This started me on a road of wagging school, smoking pot, hitch hiking, having sex, drinking – even to the point where I had brought Vodka to school in my water bottle. Things had gone in a downwards spiral very quickly, very dramatically. I was not in a good way.

Things at home were the worst they had ever been. Mum and dad just fought, day in day out. Both mum and dad at that stage were on a disability pension from Centrelink. Dad was very cunning and would go down to the bank really early in the morning on payday and get all the money out of the bank so that he could have complete control over it all during the fortnight. He would make mum almost beg for money, even for groceries, and then she would have to bring back the change and the receipt so that he could check what she was buying. He wouldn't even let her buy new $10 bras when she needed them; we had to offer mum our pocket money so that she could get some, as hers were so old they had holes in them. Dad suffered from depression, but at this point wasn't on any medication for it, so he was not the easiest of people to live with. He made mum's life hell, and would try to do the same to us, but mum tried hard to keep us out of it, and for that I'm grateful.

It was so horrible to be at home, so I stayed out late at friends' houses or just wandered around the neighbourhood, keeping as far away from WW3 as I could. They'd do it behind closed doors most of the time, but we always knew what was going on.

There was never any physical violence, but the mental and psychological abuse that I saw my dad doing to my mum was heartbreaking because I felt I couldn't do anything about it. I started sticking up for mum and back chatting my dad, becoming a little bit aggressive towards him because I didn't like to see what he was doing. Mum grew more and more hunched over and quiet each day, which was totally not like her. She'd always been the strong one, but it was almost like he got enjoyment out of crushing her spirit.

I'd discovered that I could temporarily fill that hole in my heart with affection from men, albeit only because they wanted something, but for me at the time it was enough. I knew that what I was doing was wrong and that I was allowing myself to be used, but at that point I really didn't give a toss. I just wanted a little bit of something, a smidgen of happiness, even for a short time, and was resigned to get it any way I could. I'd missed out on so many years of affection that I was starved of it. Like a homeless person going through the garbage to find food, I did whatever I could to satisfy that basic need for love and affection. Deep down I knew I was just a plaything, but for just that moment I felt needed, and that was enough.

I moved out of home and into my boyfriend's parents' place as soon as I turned sixteen; I couldn't *wait* to get out of there! I was so excited to leave the fighting and negativity, but didn't realise that I was putting myself into a situation where there were little to no rules and therefore I was digging myself into a deeper hole than I was already in. I started drinking, *a lot,* smoking pot and hanging out with degenerates. I eventually tired of the shenanigans though and ended up moving back home for a short time.

My depression had gotten so bad that I didn't want to even live anymore; there didn't seem to be any point in going on as the darkness had overtaken me. Home life was awful, school was horrendous, and I felt I had no one I could really talk to. I'd heard mum talking about ways to commit suicide when she was discussing some counselling she had been doing, and had heard her talking about people drinking whole bottles of Panadol and it just putting them into a sleep that they didn't wake up from. This idea sounded better and better to me each day. I bought two bottles, just to be sure, and walked just down the road to the local park and sat on the swings there, ready to end the misery. As I was about to open the first bottle an amazing thing happened...a butterfly came floating past and then landed on my arm, the one holding the bottle of Panadol. It just sat there, as if it was looking at me, pleading with me not to go through with it. It was as if this amazing creature had come along to let me know that no matter how bad things get, there is always something beautiful to look forward to. I believe this was Spirit that day, one of my angels sending me a sign. I dropped the bottle and just cried and cried like I've never cried before. I cried rivers that day; everything that I'd been holding in for years and years came flowing out of me. It was great to let out all those previously unshed tears. Mum always taught me not to cry, to be "tough" as if there was some kind of medal for not showing your emotions, but it was like I had opened up a well of emotions and tears and everything came flooding out. I cried for what felt like hours before heading home, with a slightly renewed sense of self.

Not too long after this, I met Jack* through an online chat while I was staying at my friend's place. This was when the internet first really became popular, and my mum hated the idea of me being able to talk to people from all over the country and the world. Being a parent myself now, I can of course understand why. We spoke literally all night and I felt an immediate connection. I kept in contact with him over the next few weeks and we decided that we would like to meet and that I would go and visit Jack on his farm. This meant a road trip, as he lived quite a distance away, but I loved the idea of getting away from it all again as nothing had really changed at home; if anything it had gotten worse.

I didn't tell my parents where I was going or when, as I knew that they would not let me leave. So I decided to just pack a bag one night, walked up the road and caught the bus to the train station very early the next morning. I left a note saying where I was going, and assuring them not to worry. I said I would be fine and asked them not to try to contact me. Of course they didn't listen to that nonsense and called the police to report me missing. The police contacted me and then came out to the farm to check on me and encouraged me to go home, but I was safe and not in any danger, so (I'm assuming with my mother's permission) they let me stay there.

I visited Jack for three weeks, and fell into a teenage version of love. At seventeen years old, you really have no idea what love is all about, but I thought I knew everything, as teenagers do. All I wanted was to be with Jack, away from the tension hanging so thick in the air, and I was going to do anything and everything in my power to make it so. Being the determined female that I am, I made it happen. I had a lovely time there; it was so peaceful and the energy was gentle and refreshing; walking through the bush each day renewed me at a deep soul level. It definitely helped clear the dark fog that had been around me, reconnecting me to Mother Earth and her healing energies. It was exactly what I needed at the time without a doubt. I'd become so negative and constantly depressed that it was great to feel a bit of light back in my life. I soaked it all up like a sponge, enjoying the atmosphere, free of negativity and criticism.

I went back home for a couple of weeks, and made plans to move in with Jack, against my parents' wishes, but at that point I was so fed up with the negative and draining energy at home that I didn't care who I upset; I just wanted out of there. I think maybe if things hadn't been so bad at home, I wouldn't have been so keen to move so far away, but I do believe it was a factor in my decision to go. It was almost as if I had manifested someone living so far away, so that I could physically remove myself from the destructive situation at home.

So off I went on what felt like an adventure at the time. It felt like a new start for me. I was hoping that it would be the end to my self-destructive ways as well, and an end to the black cloud that seemed to hover over me constantly.

We lived together for around a year on Jack's parents' farm, until we decided that it was time for us to have a place of our own and we ended up moving to the farm next door, into a little mud brick house.

I became pregnant not too long after we'd moved out, which I was actually pretty happy about – even at seventeen – but Jack was not impressed. He said he wasn't ready for it and gave me an ultimatum of keeping either the angel growing inside of me, or keeping our relationship. That was an easy choice to make, and I duly left him to move back home with my parents.

Just a few months after Tim* was born, I met Craig* online. We met properly and began a relationship, which ended up being mentally abusive, a carbon copy of what my mother had been through in that regard. We split up and got back together every second week, constantly arguing and screaming at each other, fighting over trivial things. Nothing I did was ever good enough and I was made to feel as if no one would ever want me except him because I had a child. Craig had me so brainwashed that I believed whatever came out of his mouth. He lived with his parents without a job, even in his late 20's, and it was always a bone of contention that he wouldn't move in with me, but I fell for his lies when he said that he would move in with me when we had an angel of our own. I fell pregnant again very soon after making this decision, but when Trevor* was born, I was still living on my own with two angels to raise. We fought back and forth and eventually split up for around twelve months, before getting back together again. This time it didn't last very long, as I had gained some self-confidence during the time apart and didn't put up with his crap anymore, so we broke up for good this time. However, in the short time we had been together, I had started growing another angel in my belly.

My mum decided not long before Kate* was born to leave my dad, and she lived with us for six months, before moving into her own place. After she moved out, I had no help from anyone; I was doing everything on my own. Tim had been diagnosed with ADHD (Attention Deficit Hyperactive Disorder), Trevor was currently undiagnosed but would later be diagnosed with Autism, and I had a new baby Kate, who would later be diagnosed with ADHD and ODD (Oppositional Defiance Disorder) as well. So to say it was a handful would be an understatement. I know that there are a lot of other women in similar situations doing it so hard or even harder, but it was bloody hard work. I was studying, working part time and raising my three angels, all at the same time. This didn't leave a lot of time for me.

I asked and asked both my parents often to help me out with the kids and to have them overnight occasionally so that I could have a break, but it was rarely that I had a child free night altogether. Mum would often have Tim for one night most weekends, but I always had the other kids at home. It just seemed I never got even five minutes just for me.

My Asperger's had really started to become a problem, and I also started showing signs of OCD (Obsessive Compulsive Disorder), cleaning the house and needing to have everything *just right*. This became my coping mechanism – having the house clean and tidy – and I started to drink again on a regular basis.

I had always been car mad, a Holden girl at heart, so when I met Frank* through my brother who owned a business restoring and doing up cars, I thought I'd hit the jackpot! I had spoken to him a few times, and he'd always seemed like quite the gentleman. He had done our family quite a few nice favours, and seemed like a genuinely good guy, so I decided to start seeing him.

Things between us were fairly good at the time, but there was one day when Kate was playing near a cupboard with a child safety lock on the inside of the door. She was jumping around near it, so Frank yelled out

"Hey! Get away from there, don't be so stupid!" All I heard was *stupid* and it was as if a rage boiled up instantly within me. It brought back all those years of mum calling me stupid, and I lost the plot. I screamed like a banshee at him, yelling "Don't you call my kid stupid! She's not stupid!!" and was crying and just a big mess really. He was only trying to stop her from hurting herself, but that word triggered a protective instinct inside me more strongly than I had ever felt before. No one was going to put my child through the same thing that I went through.

This was the turning point, the moment I came crashing down, the beginning of my mental breakdown.

Over the next month or two I was all over the place; I couldn't sleep, couldn't eat, and was drinking a lot again. I don't even remember half of what went on at the time. I started seeing a psychiatrist at the hospital who prescribed me Xanax, an anti-anxiety medication, and my GP had given me sleeping medication and anti-depressants as well. I was also seeing a psychologist, but nothing seemed to be helping me at that time.

Things got to the point where that black cloud was hanging too heavy over my head, and it seemed as though no matter how many times or how much I pleaded, no one seemed to want to help me. I felt that I had to take drastic action to get some assistance, so that's what I did. I took my new prescription of Xanax, parked the car down the road next to the lake, and took about 6 or 7 of them. I knew they would be enough to make me pretty sleepy and slurry when I spoke, but not enough to do any real damage. I then called Frank and told him that I'd taken a handful of pills and wanted to end it all. He called the ambulance and they called me, wanting to know where I was so that they could help me. I ended up telling them where I was and Frank came and drove me to the hospital.

I ended up staying in the hospital for a few days, and the hospital contacted the Department of Community Services (DOCS) for the safety of the children, as they have to by law in instances such as this. Surprisingly, I wanted this; it was what I had been aiming for, finally getting someone to help me, finally getting some acknowledgment that I needed assistance. I spoke to DOCS to try and get some help with the kids, some respite or advice on how to help handle the kids. I was really trying to do the right thing and change for the better. They ended up asking me if I'd be willing to let mum take care of the kids for three months while I got myself sorted out, and that if I needed another three months after that, then they'd organise that as well. This seemed like a reasonable thing at the time, as something definitely needed to change, so I went ahead with their idea and the kids went to stay with her while I saw professionals to try and gain some traction on my recovery.

The sleeping medication I'd been prescribed had been known to cause blackouts, and I'm fairly certain this had been happening to me. I would be driving and not remember getting there and that sort of thing. It wasn't until later on that I knew this was a known side effect of using this medication. So while I was trying to get better, to clear my head and work through some of the trauma I'd been through in my life, this was holding me back.

After the three months DOCS had given me to get help, they decided that I hadn't made enough progress for their liking, regardless of the fact that the sleeping medication had been hampering my efforts, and took custody of my three children. It was the worst day of my existence.

We went through court and I had to jump through various hoops, but eventually they agreed to a plan to have the kids back into my care full time. However, during the time the kids had been out of my care, I'd still been seeing Frank, and he had been both physically and mentally abusing me in the meantime. There was one instance not long after the kids started coming back to see me, when he arrived at my house and I had a male friend there. Frank was a very jealous and untrusting man, so regardless of the fact that there was nothing going on between us, he assumed that there was. He lost his cool and pretty much kicked the door in, violently attacked my friend and then started laying into me. He back handed me so hard that I hit the floor, where he proceeded to kick me in the stomach. He choked me several times; just before I was passing out he would stop. A few times I did pass out and he'd slap my face so that I'd snap out of it. I thought I was going to die that night, and I almost did. There were 22 phone calls to the police that night. They charged through the door and arrested him, literally saving my life. I thank God for each and every person that called that night; they were my angels, as much as the police themselves were.

Frank was a loving and gentle man when you were on his good side, but being on his bad side was never a good place to be. So I had to make the hardest decision I'd ever had to make, and let the kids stay in my mum's custody, where they'd be safe from harm. I'd had people following me and attempting to break into my house, cars broken into and things moved around; they were simply letting me know that they could get to me. I just couldn't let the kids be in that kind of unsafe environment, so I told DOCS that I couldn't go through with the kids coming back. I would much rather have them safe, than to be with me in what could have been a very dangerous situation.

Life and time doesn't stop for anyone; it still goes by regardless of what things we go through, and so I had to learn to live my life without the kids with me 24/7. I was very lucky in the fact that my mum had custody of the kids rather than a foster family and she was always open to me visiting them whenever I wanted, so I have always had regular contact. It took me a long time to get used to the fact that I wasn't going to have the kids waking me up each morning. Life was always so quiet and dull. I missed my babies so much, and hated having to say goodbye to them each time I'd take them home. It was like leaving a piece of my heart there.

*******

After years of being on anti-depressants and seeing psychologists, I slowly gained some insights and grew as a person. I started to learn to love myself, accept myself and forgive myself. I had to accept that I was doing the best job I could at the time, but now I knew better. I'd been abused in so many different ways, brainwashed and victimised. I now chose to put all of that garbage behind me and make better choices now that I had learnt and had some respect for myself. I wasn't allowing others to use me; I showed myself compassion and love, and in turn was able to show the kids more love and patience.

I eventually met a decent man, a loving, kind and honestly gentle man. A man who would do anything for me, and would give up everything he had on this earth just to be with me. Seth* was the epitome of everything I had ever wanted in a husband and then some. We were together for a couple of years before he asked for my hand in marriage. It was a beautiful, romantic proposal that I'll never forget. I've had so many wonderful times with Seth; never in my lifetime had I thought that I could be so happy and *genuinely* loved. Not loved for what I could do for him, but just loved for being me. I could be honest and open with him in every way, and he never made me feel bad for anything; he was just there for me 100%.

Seth was really the turning point for me in my life. He gave me so many compliments which helped give me the self-confidence that I needed to learn to love myself again. In turn, this gave me the love I needed to give to others, my kids especially. Before meeting Seth I'd almost gotten to the point where I thought they'd be better off without me in their lives, but he helped me to see what a positive influence I was on them now. They looked forward to spending time together with Seth and me, just being together enjoying each other's company.

Seth introduced the kids to camping, being outdoors, responsibility, love and being a dad. The kids have never really had their fathers in their lives, so it was a new concept for them, which they all appreciated and thoroughly enjoyed. He's taken these angels into his heart and really and truly cares for them as if they are his own. There are not a lot of men that I know that would accept the situation as it is and be so supportive.

I had started going to a Christian church, as I had felt a deep longing for some spiritual connection, something more. However, I found the church members quite two faced. They would preach one thing but do another, so I kept on looking for something that would satisfy me on a soul level.

I discovered a Spiritual Centre that did some meditations and classes, and quite enjoyed what I found there. The people there were really supportive of one another. The meditations and classes helped me learn a lot about myself, my emotions, and my needs and how to achieve what I wanted by the way that I thought. They put me on the path of self-healing through connecting with my spirit guides, my angels and God. It was through this time that I worked through some of the old hurts and abuse to finally put them to rest. I learnt to forgive those that had hurt me so that I didn't bring that pain with me to the future.

I learnt about the Law of Attraction, where you manifest things in your life, both good and bad, by your thoughts, words and actions. This made so much sense to me! All those times where I'd been in a negative head space had brought me only more negativity and bad experiences. When I met Seth and started being more positive and happy in general, life got better and better for me as time went by. So I practised this; I tried it out for myself.

The first thing I tried was a simple one. It was raining one day when I needed to go to the shops, so I asked the angels to provide me with a car space undercover near the entry so that I didn't have to get wet. I imagined the empty space that I wanted in my mind; I pictured what it looked like in my imagination. Lo and behold, as I drove into the car park, the space that I'd pictured was empty! I laughed and thought maybe it was a coincidence, but I tried it time and time again, and every single time it would work. So I started using this strategy with other more important areas of my life.

I created some posters and placed on them pictures and words describing things that I wanted to manifest. Some of those things have happened for me already, and some of them are in the process of manifesting for me right now. I've been amazed and pleasantly surprised with what I have been able to bring into my life in this way.

I've always had a deep yearning to be in a profession where I'm helping people. I never knew *what* I wanted to do; just that I wanted to make a positive difference in people's lives. I have tried various jobs and tried to make a difference in what I was doing, but nothing really satisfied me, or was really making much of a difference in the way that I really wanted.

Through the Spiritual Centre, I learnt the healing mode called Reiki. It is an energy based healing, working on unblocking and clearing the 7 main chakras in your body. I completed the first two of the three levels while going to this Spiritual Centre, which enabled me to be able to practise Reiki professionally. I kept thinking to myself that one day I'd open a Reiki business, but then I thought to myself, "What exactly is it that I'm waiting for? When is this "one day" going to happen?" So I decided that it was going to be *that* day! I applied for the business name, got myself an Australian Business Number, created a Facebook page and that was it, done!

It was as simple as putting one foot in front of the other. The biggest challenge, though, was having the courage to know that I was good enough, that I would succeed. All of my practising of the Law of Attraction was really coming into play now. I knew that if I pictured myself succeeding in this business, that was exactly what would happen, and it did.

I have a successful Reiki business which gives me such a joy and satisfaction that I never knew would be possible. I also give spiritual guidance and lessons that touch people in such a positive and lovely way. I'm finally in the exact place that I'm meant to be spiritually. I feel such a deep connection to spirit and Mother Earth now that I'm on my soul path. I get beautiful words of thanks for everything I do. I am shown appreciation and love in return for the effort I put in, which is a lovely compliment and acknowledgement that I'm doing the right thing.

Every day for me now is all about love, laughter, positivity and bringing light into my own and others' lives. If I can make one person smile or feel a little happier each day, I know I've done well. Don't get me wrong; I have my crappy days just as everyone else does, bad things still happen to me – that's just life – but I know that I have it within me to bring about positive changes. If I don't like what's happening in my life, I know I can turn it around. It's a very powerful concept, one that took me a long time to completely understand and trust in, but it is a concept that hasn't failed me yet.

Another thing that I've learnt through my spiritual journey is the power of gratitude. While things may not be perfect, sometimes they may be absolutely awful, but there is always something to look forward to or be thankful for. Sometimes it may even just be the fact that you woke up that morning, just that you're alive!

As I started being more thankful for what I had, rather than concentrating on or worrying about what I didn't have, more positive people and abundance flowed freely into my life, and still do.

*******

I am grateful for the opportunity to share my story with you. I hope that it reaches out and shows you that no matter how bad things get, how deep in the hole you seem to be, there is always light. There is always hope that things can get better, and *you* have the power within you to make that happen. You hold the key to your heart's desires; maybe you just didn't realise it was in your own hand all along.

Various Authors

# Mama J's Healing Therapies

Reiki - In person and by distance

Clairvoyant/Tarot Readings - Via email

mamajshealingtherapies@live.com

www.facebook.com/mama.js.healing.therapies

## About Jodie Freeman

Jodie currently resides on the coast of NSW, Australia. She is married to a wonderful, supporting husband and is a mother to her beautiful children. She enjoys reading and writing, spending time in nature (especially by the water), camping with the family, learning about different aspects of spirituality and creating her Aboriginal artworks.

Jodie plans to write books about her spiritual journey, learn Hypnotherapy and Past Life Regression and eventually have a Spiritual Retreat on a farm, where people can come to rejuvenate and heal.

Various Authors

# The Healing that comes After Death

### Written by Kylie Young

Every time I sit down to write, I look at the blank screen and think, 'where do I start?' My mind is calm. My heart feels healed. My body feels good and my soul shines through. So why do I stop myself from the first paragraph? Because I am dyslexic. I put my own mental block into action and I block my own flow. Recently I find myself becoming very addicted to the power of prayer, mediation, affirmations and connecting to my soul team to help me tell my story.

This morning I sat in the room at hospice, watching my granddad sleep. He looked so peaceful. My inner voice took over and asked me to 'hold his hand, let him know you are here'… so I sat watching him and this song came on TV in Maori

| | |
|---|---|
| E tangi ana koe | You are weeping |
| Hine e hine | Little girl, darling girl |
| E ngenge ana koe | you are weary |
| Hine e hine | Little girl, darling girl |
| Kati tō pouri rā | Be sad no longer |
| Noho i te aroha | There is love for you |
| Te ngākau o te Matua | in the heart of the Father |
| Hine e hine | Little girl, darling girl |

I sat for a few moments in tears. The song was sung in Maori but I knew the meaning from when I was doing my teacher training. My mum arrived in the room and then elders from the church came and served granddad sacrament and left again. Some time was spent discussing the material aspects of our day and our lives and then mum felt prompted to tell her father how much gratitude she had for him. I sat and observed one of the most beautiful communications I think I will ever see in this lifetime. Too special for me even to put words to, right now. Due to me finding my soul truth I am now rewarded with seeing faith and our heavenly father's work in action.

But this isn't to be a story of my granddad; it is my story... one of marriage, love, children, loss of two beautiful babies, separation, heart ache, and then starting my journey to find the light within. I am quite a humorous person by nature so I am hoping some of that will come through in my story.

At the age of 17, I met my soul mate; he wore the cutest little black jeans and we had an instant connection of friendship, I had this real attraction to him and I just wanted to know more. By the time I had met him I had already left home, rebelled from my parents' wishes and desires for me and, biggest of all, I ran from my faith and religion. I was raised in a Mormon family, and now I know that my years in the religion give me the foundation for now. My path and journey and life were to be different from those of my brothers and sisters from when I was born. Releasing all the fear I had for 20 or so years that I had mentally built up was the key for me to making this realisation. Then my confirmation was in a blessing my granddad gave me as a teenager which I only came across recently.

Colin and I ran into confrontation from the word go; Colin is Chinese and I am European. So it was massive for the oldest son to be even contemplating a white girl let along marrying her! It was our pure love for each other that got us through and kept us strong and committed. I did a four month trip to the States on a summer camp in Connecticut, all on my own at the age of 19. That time was so hard on both Colin and I; we had massive phone bills and there was no Skype or Facebook in those days! Upon my return we got engaged and after planning my dream wedding we decided to elope to Fiji. No family was there to witness our marriage; I had held onto so much guilt and hurt about this for way too long. It is my dream to dress my daughter on her wedding day and I took that away from my mum. But I know she understood, because of her faith. Colin and I saved and bought our first home and having a family seemed like the natural progression for me, but Colin's desire was more to travel. So we made a 6 month pact; if I fell pregnant within 6 months we would have a family, if not we would travel the following year. I fell pregnant in month 6!

Our first son was born in September 2001. Aiden was a sleepy baby and a very active toddler; he was the child that used to like tasting other children at playgroup, or exploring movements with his arms in the directions of other children. I remember clearly thinking when he was 3 that this was one difficult child to love. But he is the greatest blessing in life and the child who has taught me unconditional love. He has the best sense of humour that could make me smile no matter how depressed I was.

Our second son Ryan was born in May 2003. He was my 'dream' baby and toddler. He brought us pure love and light; he slept 4 hours during the day between feeds and slept through the night from about 5 weeks old.

After the birth of Ryan depression affected me; but I look back to that time and wonder if my issue was more that I was lacking the tools to cope with my children. But not once did I ever stop to give gratitude for these two gorgeous boys that I had been blessed with. I wanted more – I wanted the best house, and I wanted Colin to have the best job and earn the most he could. But not once did I say 'thank you' to our heavenly father for giving me such blessings.

Life was lived in a cloud but I knew it was up to me to get me out of it. I was, however, lacking that knowledge on how to do it. I tried to trust my intuition even though it was quite clouded. I needed to keep my mind busy so I started studying extramurally and began my Diploma in Teaching for early childhood education. Soon after starting I found out I was pregnant with my third child. I met this news with some apprehension. I was not coping that well with the demands of the boys. The weeks started to tick by and at 10 weeks, I started to bleed one evening. My heart sank; I didn't know really what it meant. After a quick call to the midwife she arranged for me to go up to hospital in the morning unless things got worse during the night. At 3am I woke up with labour like pains and then I felt a 'pop' sensation. I went to the bathroom and it didn't look good. In tears I went back to bed and cuddled up with Colin. The next morning we headed up to hospital.

At the hospital I chatted with the lady and she said that it certainly sounded like I had miscarried but she would do a scan to make sure there wasn't any 'products' left behind. To our shock there was a happy little baby bouncing around in my tummy, very active and very happy. The bleeding had stopped, so I got a 'congratulations ... it can be normal to bleed in early pregnancy.' I was very shocked, but I felt 'wow this is meant to be,' so I got quite excited and started planning more for the baby's arrival. I got to about 19.5 weeks and I had just dropped the boys to day care so that I could go home and study. But once again I felt that similar sensation of fluid gushing... so I quickly made my way home.

I was bleeding again and I made the call to the midwife and Colin. My midwife arrived and was just sitting with me discussing what to do when my waters broke. I just cried because I knew it wouldn't be good for the baby if I had to deliver the baby then. We couldn't hear a heartbeat through the Doppler. Colin and I headed to the hospital and waited for many hours up there. When I was seen the doctor was very 'clinical' and just sent us home again with antibiotics and told us what would happen from here if the baby was alive. I would be in hospital on antibiotics till I was 26 weeks. The baby was going to be very premature. He explained the health complications to the child. We had to go back the next day for an ultrasound.

That night I felt so alone and empty; nothing brought me comfort. I cried and even saying goodnight to the boys was an effort. Colin tried talking to me but I shut him out as well. I prayed and asked that our heavenly father make the best choice for our baby. The next day I felt guilty for asking this. My mum picked me up in the morning and we headed back up to hospital. Everyone spoke to me so softly and just got me up for the scan. Soon we saw the baby on the screen and there was no life, but the stenographer still got a second opinion. We cried quietly and I messaged Colin, 'the baby has gone.'

He was already in the process of making his way up to us and he just flew into my arms when he saw me. I quickly learnt that there was no 'protocol' for a second trimester loss. They preferred I delivered the baby up in the wards but the ward was full, so then they rang the delivery suite to see if they could accommodate me. I was lucky a midwife there was prepared to look after me for the day as the delivery suite wasn't the most ideal place for me to be, so the staff midwifes kept telling me.

I was settled into a room in the delivery suite and the staff midwife started to talk to me about how they were going to induce labour. I thought it was going to be similar to my inductions with Aiden and Ryan, but it wasn't. They used the drug that they use in terminations to get things underway. Because there was no set protocol in place, the paperwork they used and the forms I had to sign were all for a 'termination of pregnancy'.

Contractions started slowly and my awesome midwife rang to see how I was going. She decided to head up and support me for that end stage, which to be honest, didn't last too long. So with my mum, Colin, midwife, student midwife and staff midwife present, my baby was born! She was so developed – fingers, toes, nose, eyes... just like the pregnancy book said she would. I asked if anyone could see a 'physical' reason why she died and there was none. I got about half an hour with her and then the box was brought in; I could take her straight home with me. Jaimie Kylie Young, born 29 September 2004.... She fitted perfectly in my hands no bigger than a block of butter. She is with my Granny now in the spirit world, and that seemed to give me some comfort.

The days that followed were a blur; my mum and dad organised a funeral for her. The service was beautiful and so many people came to show their support for Colin and me. My milk still came in. I cried day and night. I couldn't take any joy in my boys who constantly fought. I was angry, hurt and numb. I didn't understand 'why'. I blamed Colin for a long time and I really had no real reason for this. It was because my mind told me to.

Days kept happening and the weeks kept ticking by and everyone said maybe having another baby might help heal the open wound that was left. I waited till all the tests were back from Jaimie. There was nothing wrong physically or genetically. The doctor said, 'it was just some bad luck, but don't worry, when this happens it is generally a one off.' So strangely I took some comfort from that and Colin and I started trying again.

In July 2005 I found out I was pregnant again! I met this news with quite a bit of nervousness, but the same nausea inflicted me hard as it did with Jaimie. I got to 10 weeks pregnant; I had a bit of spotting but the baby was ok. I was extremely anxious and nervous now! I knew in my gut things weren't right. When I was 16 weeks pregnant I started to relax somewhat and went swimming with my kids at the pools on a Saturday (but later found out I shouldn't have done that). On Sunday morning I woke up and went to the toilet. I was standing at the basin and looked down; I was standing in a pool of blood. I screamed for Colin and he did not know what to do. My midwife was in a delivery, so she said to put a pad on and if it got worse to head straight up to hospital but otherwise wait for her to come over. She got to me at about 4pm; she put the Doppler on and we heard a heartbeat. I really felt things were going to be different this time!

My mum accompanied me to the hospital as we felt leaving Colin with the boys was the best option. I wasn't in Emergency department long when I felt as if I had passed something. I was bleeding heavily and the doctors responded quickly. She was the sweetest doctor; she put a speculum in to have a look to see if my cervix had dilated, and she spent ages just looking. Then she looked up at me with her eyes welled up and said, 'I am sorry Kylie, when I put the speculum in and opened it up the baby just popped out at me.' I remember just saying 'no…. no … no… not again.'

Colin came up when I was settled in the wards; he didn't know really what to say to me and nor did I. I just stared out the window and whenever someone new came into the room I cried again. I didn't want to feel anything; I didn't want to acknowledge what had just happened. I just wanted to ignore what had happened. Cameron was born on the 16 October 2005. We had a small service for him with just my immediate family. I just didn't want to accept that I was dealt this set of cards again! I was fairly angry and yelling at God for punishing me again. I was angry at Colin for not being there for me, for being so distant from me. My mind started playing games with me again.

Because I was in ignore mode, getting on and having another baby just seemed logical. But I knew I needed some help as the medical profession offered me no answers. So I went and saw our local acupuncturist, a little older Chinese lady. She was one of the few that made me smile again. She said to me 'your ying and yang are all ova the place… I fix.' So for the next 3 months I went once a week whilst she balanced my body. I think she put a few 'happy' needles in as well. I was feeling awesome! I took joy in my boys again, and enjoyed taking them to the park, playing with them and just being a mum! The simple joys of life were coming back to me. One month after finishing my treatment I fell pregnant again! I was finally learning the advantage of living a positive life.

I will never forget a friend saying, 'aren't you done torturing yourself?' but I knew I had it in me and I knew I could do it. I had to promise Colin that this was it, but no matter what the outcome, he was done. He couldn't handle the roller coaster anymore. The first 12 weeks went by without any problem – I had no sickness, just tiredness. At 12 weeks I had a small bleeding, just a couple of spots of blood. I went through the procedure and the scan showed a happy bouncy baby. But thoughts turned to saving this baby and doing all I could. The doctors suspected that maybe I had an incompetent cervix, so I was put on 'light duties' and I had fortnightly scans until the baby was born just to monitor things. Would you believe it, I made it to term! One week before her due date my waters broke which did not trigger labour and I was induced with her.

Sarah-Grace was born on 8 August 2007. But something happened somewhere during her birth that led her to get very sick. My baby came home, but her umbilical cord just didn't want to heal. Initially I dismissed it because I remembered the boys' cords getting a tad yucky and I knew the midwife would be visiting the next day.

Sarah-Grace ended up in hospital because she was only a week old. She was not responding to antibiotics and she also had no white blood cells to fight the infection. Sarah-Grace got very sick very quickly. That was the time when I remembered my faith. Man did I pray? I prayed the hardest I ever have in my whole life, and also apologised for my anger and lack of faith.

Sarah-Grace had an ultrasound in the afternoon and by the time I got up to the ward with her the surgeons had decided to operate on her. The swab from the area indicated a bacterium that was related to faecal matter. The surgeons felt that her bowels and umbilical cord didn't seal off at birth. The risks were explained to me but I felt that the doctors were making the best choice for her. I tried calling Colin as I was told to say my 'goodbyes' because the anaesthetic alone held some risk. But the staff moved really fast. I felt so alone at the waiting room by the theatre, seeing the doctor take her from me. I sat and cried! My baby girl please make it!

She did make it through surgery. However, in recovery she wasn't responding the way they wanted to. So the call was made to bring me into the room to see if that would help. I picked up this blue looking baby and as soon as she was in my arms, the crying calmed and her colour returned. The bond between me and her was clearly very strong!

We spent a number of weeks in hospital with her; we seemed to pick up every bug going through the ward, so she ended up in isolation for the last 2 weeks. Once we were all under one roof I couldn't relax with Sarah-Grace. I wanted to wrap her in cotton wool. I started my obsessions with washing my hands; I didn't like visitors holding her or touching her just in case she got sick. I did quite a bit of cognitive therapy to help me overcome this. But over the years I had built up quite a bit of resentment towards Colin, mainly for just not being there when I needed him. I was angry because work, running and friends came before me.

I immersed myself in things that distracted me from just 'being' in the moment with my family. I lived on the computer, talking to friends on messenger or facebook. I finished my Diploma, reconnected with old friends and chatted to them about their own lives and helped them whenever I could. I knew I loved my kids but I was mentally preparing myself for the day they died, because I seriously believed that they would be taken from me.

Colin picked up the pieces with the kids where he could, but he let me go off in whatever tangent I wanted to go in. That made me feel he just didn't care anymore. But that was my life at home; I came across more focused on my job, not my inner turmoil that was going on. But breaking point came because leading two lives really wasn't serving to the true me. But who was the true me? I decided I wanted to be happy; I didn't want this for me anymore.

With no skills (or so I thought) I started to think my way through changing my life so that I could feel happy again. Since the person that annoyed me the most was Colin, leaving him seemed like the thing I should do for me to be happy! So that's just what I did, and man, did I come under fire from family and friends! I wasn't prepared for the loneliness on my own; I thought I would love having a quiet home, but those voices in my head were even louder. Our children were in shared care, one week about. I loved my week with those kids. I taught them manners and to have respect for what they had. Believe me, it wasn't all roses and I had some challenges with them but mostly it was good.

My first week alone was the hardest week; it was my birthday on the Sunday and it seemed everyone abandoned me. I turned to the internet for comfort. I had a quick look at a dating site. I had no deliberate intention of making contact but all of a sudden some messages started coming through. So I got talking to one person in particular called Matt.

He told me he had some abilities to read scenarios, that he was able to talk with people that had passed over and that he had some healing gifts as well. I was so smitten and taken with his 'gifts' that I didn't listen to the inner guidance that he wasn't right for a relationship with me. I can still remember that internal kick I felt when things started to progress from a friendship, but I ignored it because I was lonely.

The relationship we had was one full of arguing, emotional abuse and fear and he had this pull on me that I felt it so hard to get out of. But yet I don't want to focus on the negatives that happened, the loss of money, friends and the respect of my family, and the mess he left me in.

My lowest point happened one night. I was going to end my life; I was done with feeling hurt. I started walking and without realising it, I was at Colin's house. I had a massive chat with Colin who was reluctant to let me go home. I was worried for his safety if Matt came looking for me. Instead I went and I sat on the river bank. My mind couldn't get past the inner voice which said, 'your kids need a mum.' It was enough to pull me through.

My plan changed (those that know me well know that my indecisiveness is intolerable, but its way better now); my journey to a better life started. I gave up paid employment. I started to realise that I needed to surround myself with things I was passionate about, not worry about the material stuff so much anymore. Matt and I broke up for the final time and he moved to another town; we still remained good friends until he left New Zealand to return to his home country. But I now realised he was still controlling me and using his abilities to stop me gaining strength in my journey. His tactics were subtle but it is only now that I can see them. My focus changed to my children and I tried to make sure that they were balanced in their mind, body and soul. I can officially say that this was one massive hill to climb to gain back the respect of my children for tearing apart our family and putting a person in my life that they were never comfortable with. Ryan was the only one that could see Matt wasn't what he said he was; he just seemed to intuitively know that Matt was using his abilities for self-reward and manipulation.

I immersed myself with my children and I admit that I bribed them to behave – brought them cool gadgets. But yet I was still missing the point. I cannot recall the time when I had my 'ahhh ha' moment about the kids being a mirror of me. If I am balanced in my mind, body and soul then they will naturally be as well. During this time I had terrible anxiety, fear and worry. If there was anything I could worry about I did; I over thought everything. In the evening I would have two or three glasses of wine to soften the thought processes. I wasn't comfortable being on my own, and that really stressed me. Colin was trying hard to move on with his life and quite often had me texting or ringing during the night if things got too bad for me. I was at my worst in the weeks the kids were with him.

I really wanted my family back, but I felt that I had burnt way too many bridges. Too many hearts had been broken and too much hurt and resentment had been built up among Colin's family that would sway him from wanting to be with me again. I talked to him in February about how I was feeling and he told me straight that he didn't want to commit to any relationship before he did his Europe trip. This was planned for June.

That night I cried myself to sleep. How was I going to cope being alone on my own for six months! My thoughts were very selfish, but yet I tried to distract my mind the best I could. I met many new men in my life, but they all seemed to come and go. There was no strong bond or connection like I had with Colin. So I concluded that I just needed to be comfortable on my own, and that I did. Anxiety in all! All I had to do was just believe!

Time when Colin was away was special; most nights I had 3 children sleeping in my bed. I made Skype calls with their daddy whenever he had a suitable internet connection and we started flirting again. Damn it, I wanted my man back and I was going to fight for him! That's exactly what I did and 3 months later we were living together as a family again.

I feel that Colin was with an uncertain heart. My issues with anxiety and the methods I used for coping were a bit much for him. He encouraged me to see a GP and she prescribed medication for me. Great, I thought! Finally I was eased of the anxiety obsessive worry. But once again this didn't work; the anxiety just got stronger and the medication was kept being increased with this. Not at any one time did any one search behind the symptom to find a cause or suggest that actually I had the power within to combat this. I was a master of disguise. I could hold together my everyday life, but evenings and weekends were very different.

During that year I was blessed to have some special people join in my life. We all came from very different backgrounds but yet we all clicked! To them I owe so much gratitude for guiding me and showing me that there is another way and the answer comes from within. They guided me to a wonderful lady Marnie McDermott who wrote a book called *Beyond Happiness*. I was very blessed that she also lived in my home town. I had 2 sessions with her and what happened in my session was very personal to me but you come away with a 'prescription'. I had daily affirmations to do 5 times a day for 3 weeks and on my next visit she channelled a message from my soul team. ***'Recipe for life':***

*Love yourself*
*Trust your guidance*
*Welcome goodness into your life*
*Love every moment*

I live my life to my recipe, also reading books to quench my thirst just wanting to know more. I searched the internet to find out more about my angels that are guiding me. I learnt to meditate on how to expand my mind. I have seen some beautiful things in meditation that inspires me to lead a positive life, filled with joy and abundance. I remember that on my second visit to Marnie she said, 'you have flicked your switch.' I was proud of how I turned things around in a relatively short period of time. I had a new addiction and that was for life.

I wrote down every fear and worry I had, and I burnt that puppy and said a healing prayer with it. Praying has come very easily to me and just believing in the universe, building a relationship with my soul team, heavenly father, god, mother divine and friend, helped give me insight into nurturing my physical body and what it was that I needed to do to keep get clearer and stronger communication with my soul team.

I don't beg for more money or a better life in my prayers and meditations; instead I give gratitude and love. I appreciate the trials and mountains that I am sent to climb. Instead of questioning why I say, 'why not'.

Negative thoughts do pop in from time to time; generally I have to sit quietly for a few minutes and give my mind a talking to. I have invested in me, with doing meditations twice a day, doing crystal therapy and having the best addiction of all, the desire to know more, to lead a positive life and to simply 'be' rather than pursue the quest to be materialistically better. My family reflect me – They are all shining so beautifully.

Life is a journey and not a destination. I am thankful for my trials for what they have taught me. I don't regret one bit of my life anymore, or worry about tomorrow. I wouldn't be the beautiful person I am now without them.

My life has changed in so many ways, listening to my soul guidance has led me to become a healer and teacher. Bring on the rest of my beautiful life!

## About Kylie Young

I was born, raised and live in Hamilton, New Zealand. I was the 4th child and I tested my parents from a very young age. I always wanted to be on my own journey. I married young and had some very special children. My children whether they are here with me physically or in heaven are so special and interact with me every day.

I lead a truly special life; I am blessed in every aspect. The journey I have lived so far could have easily defined me into a different life. But here I am, being true to my soul journey.

*A beautiful soul living a human existence.*

I hold a Diploma in Teaching for Early Childhood Education, Reiki degree and Essence of Angels (r) practitioner. I have training but yet I had the abilities within me the whole time, I just had to learn how to access them and trust.

I have a beautiful studio in my home where I work with awesome clients reconnecting their body, mind and soul. My training has taught me heaps, but using my intuition and adapting to each individual client brings the most beneficial healing.

I also love to teach, that is just what I do in my healings. I heal and teach clients tools to self heal as well. I run workshops/courses about building self confidence, parenting and understanding your body. I promote a holistic approach to removing barriers of self definitions and waking up to your own inner light.

I am a very real person, sharing my light, wisdom and love with you all

> Love 'n Light to you all on your beautiful
> journey

*Check Kylie out on facebook*
http://www.facebook.com/reikiwithatwistofme

Lead Me Guide Me Healing

Various Authors

# Through my Eyes

## Written by Claire Howard

I dedicate this story to all those who have experienced difficulty in being at peace with their true selves, all those who have lost their way in their journey through life, and all those who have forgotten their dreams, and given up hope.

I want to thank my amazing husband for his continuing devotion, his constant support in everything I do, and his deep love for me and our family.

I want to thank my beautiful friend Carmen who motivated me to write this book during a dark and difficult time in my life.

I also want to thank my very talented and supportive parents for helping with the editing and the artwork of my book.

Finally, I want to thank all of the wonderful people in my life for enriching my world with love, happiness, friendship, understanding, and respect, for each of these beautiful souls have made, and still make, a positive difference to my evolvement of self; my ongoing journey through life's ups and downs.

"I love who I am."

Can you look in the mirror and say those very words? More importantly, can you truly believe them? Imagine being that powerful, and feeling that free, knowing that you unconditionally love the beautiful person you truly are.

But before you can truly love the real you, you need to actually know who you are. And when you can do that, know who you truly are on the inside, absolutely nothing can stop you from attaining your dreams, and living your perfect life.

I am living my perfect life. And this is because I have always believed in my dreams – I have always lived in my dreams in the most positive, beautiful way. However, I have also battled some demons, and hit some very low points at different stages of my life. But each time a low came, I fought, I learned, and I picked myself up, until my inner light came back on and shone brightly again.

Nothing has ever deterred me from realising my dreams; nothing has ever deterred me from living my perfect life.

And that is what life is all about – conquering the battles, learning, picking yourself up, and letting your inner light shine again – your inner light being the real you, your true self.

I am going to take you on a journey, my journey. Through my eyes, I am going to take you through real, personal issues that so many of us encounter in life. I am going to show you how I experienced and dealt with each of these issues, in the hope of inspiring you to learn how to help yourself, and to show you how dreams, love, and positivity lead to ultimate happiness...

I was a little girl lost when we moved to this beautiful country. A little French girl arriving in such a vastly different country as Australia is a truly overwhelming experience. But the love and support of my parents and sister was protection enough, my safe haven, until school started...

And that was when my first real battle came along. It was a battle because I didn't know who I was in this foreign country, and I was so overwhelmed by this new experience that I suppressed the real me in trying to be someone who was accepted and liked by others.

Primary school was a huge learning experience – the language and the Australian culture. I did a lot of observing and absorbing during that time. But high school was the battle. I changed identity so many times. I tried to be different people to see where I fitted in – there was hippy chick Claire, homey dude Claire, skater girl Claire, preppy Claire, cutesy Claire, and I even tried to change my name to Claira. I had very low self-esteem, and consequently I denied myself the chance to let the real me shine through and evolve. And being a teenager amongst other teenagers didn't help the situation either. The incredible pressure girls are under to look a certain way can be so all consuming and destructive; it certainly consumed *me*.

With the numerous identity changes I went through came a lot of confusion, which in turn made my reality really difficult to deal with – so much so that I needed to escape all the time.

I was always trying to find a way to escape my life, whether it was seeking to be someone else, or living elsewhere. So along with escaping my life by trying to be different personas, living with people other than my family was another form of escape for me. I left home so many times in my school years, either to live with friends while their parents were away, or with boyfriends I had at the time. Leaving my parents' home gave me release from my reality, which made me feel so free.

I went through periods when I thought the whole world was against me, including my family. I changed identity and lifestyle so often that I confused my parents, and they didn't understand why their beautiful and talented daughter kept heading in the wrong direction. I lived a life of escapism and fantasy, living in my dreams. I saw my life through rose coloured glasses – a metaphor which I have since learnt that if done correctly, in a positive, realistic way, is actually one of the secrets to living your perfect life.

Another coping mechanism for me was control. When I felt my life spiralling out of control, I felt helpless, lost and afraid. I wanted to find a way to take back the reigns and regain control. I found a way...

I will always remember the day I told my sister as we sat together in our rumpus room eating lunch, "from today onwards, I will eat very slowly, so that I eat less, so that I can be skinny and therefore beautiful". I was 15 years old, and I had found a way to impose some control in my overwhelmingly confusing world.

The eating disorder I developed from that time on stayed with me for seventeen long years, until finally, as I will explain further into my story, I found a way to gain control over *it*.

An eating disorder begins with us in control, but eventually and inevitably, it ends up controlling *us*. It's a very gradual and sneaky disease, you don't realise how fast it takes control of you, of your life – where *it* has the power, and *you're* the puppet at its mercy...

So the eating disorder was my secret 'happy place' in my world of confusion. It was the only part of my life that I could control, be in charge of. It was my little secret, and the skinnier I got, the better I felt about myself.

However, there is more than one side to an eating disorder, losing weight is one, over-eating is another.

I also began to use food as a coping mechanism, and I would eat every time things got too hard for me and I couldn't cope.

My eating disorder had evolved; my world had just gotten more difficult to live in.

But, despite my lows, for all the craziness and confusion, and all the drama and the hardships they brought into my teenage years, I still saw my world through rose coloured glasses. I still very much believed I was going to have the most wonderful life, marry my prince, never have to worry about money, and have beautiful children. I also really believed I would be a star someday. But what I didn't realise back then was that I already *was* a star.

My optimism is my virtue. It doesn't matter what happens in your life, if you have an optimistic outlook, you can get through anything. If you really believe in something, anything, it will come true – one way or another, it will come true.

We are all magical beings, capable of using our power to achieve anything we want. Imagine that – having the power to achieve absolutely anything you want.

I finished school, got a couple of part-time jobs, and eventually got my first full-time office job. But my low self-esteem meant that my integration into the workforce was not a happy experience. Ultimately, twelve years of office work brought me little fulfilment, and a great deal of inner turmoil.

But amazingly, despite my internal suffering, I always made quite an impression in every office job I had. Imagine a bright, bubbly princess walking through those corporate doors, complete with sparkly eye shadow, platform shoes, and her own stash of pink stationery. This of course made me quite a standout everywhere I went. I may not have seemed the part with my eccentric look, but I was still a great worker, efficient and dedicated, and at the same time, I was loved for my ability to bring sunshine into an otherwise dull office environment.

Unfortunately, however, that life drained me, and I never understood why I just wasn't ever truly happy in any of the jobs I'd had. But this was because again, I was suppressing the real me, and denying myself the chance to really shine through. I was following, just as I did in high school, and doing what I thought I needed to do to be a normal person, like everybody else, and everybody else around me seemed to have an office job.

Eventually, after all those years working in an office environment, having analysed my strengths, weaknesses, likes and dislikes in each job I had, I realised what I needed to do. I needed to be comfortable in my working environment, I needed to be free of being stuck in the same suffocating room with the same people and I needed freedom, but also stimulation – I needed a people job. For my physical comfort, my inner peace, and my happiness, I needed to go back to a job I had been in once before, a job where I felt free to be me, to mingle with people, and a job where I did *not* have someone breathing down my neck at my every move. I needed to go back to being a 'Checkout-Chick'.

Being on my own stand-alone checkout was freedom to me – I was in control, I was in charge of my job. I was still able to utilise the processing part of my brain, which I loved, all the while being at the forefront, in direct contact with people, but never the same people, always different people passing through, keeping my job interesting.

This was my release from my feeling of entrapment in the office, and taking this step to completely change direction in my working life, to bring back peace and comfort to my soul, was taking a step to being true to me, being my true self.

Of course, some might consider a person standing behind a cash register as being in a menial position. That is judgemental and very unfair, but it actually is a true reflection of attitudes in society, and also the nature of hierarchy…

Yes, hierarchy in the workforce is a hard reality, hard because it can make people considered to be in lesser positions to feel demeaned. It can attack their self-esteem and erode their confidence. I experienced this in office jobs. Ideally, a person should have the job he/she is suited to, with no greater or lesser value attached to it, as if it were on a hierarchical continuum. But of course, we don't live in a perfect world.

Part of the key to happiness in the workforce is to be in a job that suits your personality. Be true to you, and do exactly what you want to do, because if you do, you will shine. I was desperately unhappy and felt crushed in an office, but I felt freedom, comfort and happiness in the role of a Checkout-Chick.

Interestingly, the moment I made this realisation, the moment I changed direction in my working life, amazing things started to appear in my life, truly wonderful, beautiful things. But that... comes later in my story. ☺

Working in office jobs was so unhealthy for me. While I was working, I struggled enormously with the feelings I was suppressing. My true self wanted to come out, but I was afraid, as I didn't know who my true self was, and having such low self-esteem, I probably felt my true self wasn't good enough anyway. But I wanted to be good at something, anything, and so I put my all into my work. I would go to work every day and give my job everything I had, and give myself nothing. Many a day I wouldn't eat, hardly drink, or even take a bathroom break until the end of the day. I completely suppressed my own needs for the sake of achieving, of succeeding at something. And as if this self-sacrifice during the day wasn't enough, cruelly it would then turn into punishment when I got home. I would be so hungry, so weak and completely drained, and so incredibly unhappy that the only thing that could console me was to eat; and so I ate, to fill up the void, to suppress my overwhelmingly suffocating emotions.

There have been several variations of my eating disorder, Bulimia being most consuming. Gorging myself with food would fill the hole I had inside, the emptiness, the sadness, the nothingness. And while I ate, for that brief moment, I felt safe, at peace, and happy; until of course, the end of the binge, where self-hate would raise its ugly head, and I would fill up with guilt and shame.

That cycle was so hard to break, and I took it with me everywhere I went – including into relationships. It became my coping mechanism – if I couldn't cope, I would just eat. Nothing could stop me, if I felt the need to binge, only physical force could have temporarily held me back. I was very good at hiding my illness and lying about it.

When I was in my mid-twenties, I had what is commonly referred to as a 'quarter life crisis'. I wanted freedom from my vicious cycle of pain, punishment, and self-hate, and the only thing I knew how to do was escape, and so I did. I left the life I had; I left my partner at the time, and all the material comforts that we worked for together. I left, basically with nothing but the clothes on my back.

I had often run away and started my life over again – the numerous changes of identity at school, leaving my parents' home to live with other people, leaving jobs when it all just got too much for me to handle. If I couldn't cope, I would just leave and start over again. But the life I left in my mid-twenties was the biggest escape of them all.

Leaving my partner was the right thing to do, not only because we were at different stages of our lives; sometimes love alone isn't enough. A healthy relationship also needs friendship, compatibility, and common goals. But in this case, what ultimately made me leave was the battle I had going on with myself. I was unable to function properly in the relationship because of my self-esteem issues and my eating disorder and, therefore, over time, our relationship gradually deteriorated.

The feeling I got from walking away from my life once more was exhilaration. I felt so free, so new and fresh to start again.

I began my new life with a whole new circle of friends, a new place to live, and a brand new lifestyle. I felt so alive that my eating disorder actually disappeared for a few months. I felt on top of the world. In fact, I felt so free and new that I decided to change my name. I became Emma, and I remained Emma for four years. My whole look changed too. I cut my long hair into a short pixie crop, I lost quite a bit of weight, and I changed my whole dress sense to suit my new funky self. Significantly, the only thing that didn't change, that couldn't change, was the real me. I was still me, though I tried desperately to change, to be someone new, someone better, I was still me. But of course back then, I couldn't see that, I truly believed Claire was gone and Emma had taken over. And it was this dramatic and final escape from my life that began my journey into self-discovery. This, the most extreme escapade of them all, was actually the beginning of the truth – my truth.

I learned so much from the breakup with my partner, I evolved through that experience, and as a result, I am happy to say that today, I am married to the most wonderful man. So though the breakup was one of the hardest and most painful experiences I've ever had, it was also a step in the right direction. I was evolving, and the evolving process isn't always easy or a pleasant experience. But trusting yourself, making decisions, taking action, and bringing in change will always guarantee personal evolvement, and therefore a chance for ultimate happiness.

Being Emma was such an adventure, such a learning experience, and such a blessing in disguise, literally...

As Emma I met some amazing people, some of whom remain my best friends today, and of course, I also met my soul mate, my loving husband. I had a lot of fun being Emma; I was completely immersed in my very own fantasy world. I did some crazy things, some not so good for me things, and some once in a lifetime things. I discovered within myself some of the most incredible emotions and feelings, none of which I had ever felt before in my life.

Those two years of wonderment and experimentation were a turning point for me, as that was when I discovered who the real me was – who Claire was.

Meeting my husband was one of the greatest blessings of my life. I am so incredibly lucky to have my soul mate by my side. Our connection, our commitment, and our deep love for each other have provided a solid foundation for a happy and lasting marriage. It is extremely difficult to find that special someone to share your life with, and for that someone to have the qualities a relationship needs to survive and succeed, so that you can grow together, and form a deeper, stronger, and absolutely unbreakable bond. It is difficult to find, but definitely not impossible.

Absolutely nothing in this beautiful world is impossible, because life itself is a miracle, and therefore each and every one of us is a miracle. And that in itself proves that nothing in this world is impossible.

*Positivity, optimism, and believing in your dreams – if you have all of this, you can do anything, you can create your own miracles.*

I always knew I would one day be married to my perfect man. I dreamt of a fairytale wedding, and I got my fairytale wedding. I really believed I would

*Living a Positive Life*

have it all, and I do have it all. But having said that, I also know that belief must be accompanied by guts and determination to go after what you want – and you will get it, if you truly want it, and if you work hard for it, you will get what you want.

Meeting my husband was a gift from above, a blessing, and a reward for believing so much in my dream of finding my perfect man. But our strong and unified bond, our undying love for each other, and of course, our marriage, all came not only from our hearts, but also from real commitment and determination, inspired by a desire from each of us to build a strong, loving, and blissfully happy marriage. No marriage will work, or last, without hard work. After all, we all have to work for money to guarantee financial security, which doesn't actually guarantee happiness, so why can't we also work for love, which is guaranteed to bring you the happiness your heart so desperately desires? Love is universally the one and only thing in life that will fulfil you, and truly make you happy, forever.

I have found such fulfilment as a wife. Married life, for me, is like being completely cocooned in a blanket of love, fun, and togetherness...

We got engaged in Las Vegas, in a whirlwind of love and excitement. Chris proposed on a little bridge above a canal laden with gondolas. It was the perfect romantic setting, and it made the rest of our fun-filled American holiday all the more joyous.

Planning our wedding was so exciting, a whole year of complete happiness. In fact, that year was one of the happiest years of my life. It was the year I turned 30. That year we had our engagement party, we moved into our brand new house, we had our fairytale wedding, and we went on two very different magical honeymoons – one at the beach, and one up in the mountains. Everything was perfect. 2007 will forever be imprinted in my heart; I had made my dreams a reality. I dared to dream, and I worked hard to make my dreams come true. And absolutely all of them came true!

I had found blissful happiness by taking a risk, and leaving a life that wasn't making me happy. To get my prince, my fairytale wedding, I had to go through pain and uncertainty first. Nothing is ever just handed to you on a silver platter; we all need to put in some effort towards attaining the things we desire. And to get what I desired, I had to leave a life behind.

Leaving my partner was hard – I took a huge risk, and got out of my comfort zone. I changed course, and everything changed. Sometimes all that *doesn't* glitter can actually turn into gold. That was the first real risk I took in my life. It was a risk because leaving my partner meant being on my own and starting over from scratch, and being on my own was frightening to me. But I took the risk, because I knew I had to. I knew in my heart that for the ultimate happiness of both of us, we needed to part ways.

Leaving the relationship created a domino effect that catapulted me into the first and biggest self-discovery journey of my life. And in taking that risk, by leaving my partner, and jumping on that not so glittery path on the rainbow, filled with uncertainty and fear, I still did manage to find the pot of gold at the other end – my husband.

How was I able to muster the courage to do this? Because of my dreams, my positivity, and my eternal optimistic outlook on absolutely everything I do – all my positivity far outweighed the negativity. However, with so much more life ahead of me, this pot of gold certainly didn't mean there would be no other battle to conquer, no other low point in my life, and no other risk to take. Life is not only beautiful, but it is a continual stream of challenges, and if it weren't, how would we all evolve?

My next challenge was infertility. It was something I didn't expect, a real shock to me. I had wanted to be a mother for half my life, and so I automatically thought it would just happen when I wanted it to.

Another lesson learned... Never assume, because the future isn't set in concrete; it can always change, and because it hasn't happened yet, the future you might imagine isn't actually real. I assumed my future, I assumed that conception would be natural and instant, and I got hit with a very hard slap in the face.

Worry and fear as adults: these emotions can very easily swamp our minds. We acquire these negative emotions as we grow up and absorb society's influences. Children, on the contrary, are so pure, and completely fearless. Children live for the moment, for the now, and they don't worry about the future as adults do. A lot can be learned from children. It is only when we grow up, when our minds develop and we begin to absorb and think, think some more, and over-think and analyse everything, that we begin to create our own fears and worries. And unfortunately, this is a part of human nature, a part of all of us. It is recognising this in ourselves that will enable us to take control of our thoughts, and subsequently change the way we think.

A thought is just a thought, it is not physically real. We need to recognise that since our worry or fear is just a simple thought, it's not actually real – because the event we are worrying about or fearing hasn't happened yet, and may not even happen at all. Once we've acknowledged this, we can then move on from that thought and remove all the fear or worry from our minds. So in fact, it is still possible as an adult to be fearless like a child; we just need to work harder at it.

Fear was a dominant emotion in my infertility journey; fear, worry, anger, shame and guilt, all came into play.

For over two and a half years, I battled with infertility. I gave up hope, I blamed myself, I hit very low points several times, and I asked why. How could I, someone so wanting a child, someone so full of love to bestow upon my family, not be able to fall pregnant? But despite my sorrow, despite my anger at myself and the universe, and despite my heart breaking into a million pieces, I began to fight…

The first part of my infertility journey was to heal both my mind and my body – I still had the eating disorder which I consistently fell back on to suppress the overwhelming emotions I didn't want to feel.

When we began trying for a baby I wasn't working. I was alone at home all day, glued to the computer, 'Googling' every single thing I could find on getting pregnant. And that's all I did for a couple of months, until I decided to find a part-time job to take my mind off it all.

I just couldn't understand why I wasn't falling pregnant – me, the one who wanted a baby more desperately than most people we knew, the one who everyone thought would fall pregnant straight away! It was driving me crazy, and I was just so depressed. And for a big stab in the heart on top of my already deep depression, all of our friends were falling pregnant around us – all of them without difficulty, as though it was the easiest thing in the world to do.

I started my part-time job as an Accounts Clerk, and for a while, it did take my mind off my baby sadness. That is until, just as with every other office job I'd had before, I quickly began to lose interest, and started once again to focus on getting pregnant – because in my mind, if I was pregnant, it meant I could leave my job.

This situation created such turmoil in me, turmoil which I couldn't escape. I wanted to leave work so badly, but to do that, I believed I had to actually get pregnant, which I just wasn't able to do. And because I couldn't cope at work, I would succumb completely to my eating disorder, which was the only way I knew of to numb my pain. But, of course, this then compromised my health, which in turn compromised my ability to fall pregnant. I was stuck in this vicious cycle with no way out, as I was at work every day, and so the cycle couldn't stop.

The only break I had from it all was on the weekends, when I didn't have to be at work, and therefore didn't have to suppress all my negative emotions with food. On the weekends I was free, and so the cycle would stop, and my poor little body was given a break. But two days was never enough, and by Monday afternoon I would be back to square one. I didn't know how else to control my emotions except by stuffing my mouth with food.

I was so unhappy at work, but I still put on a brave face every single day I was there. I walked into that office bright and cheery, but the beaming smile masked the pain and the sadness that I was really feeling. I had so little love for myself that I didn't allow me to feel anything. No matter what, I was going to go to work, tell myself that I was happy there, and put all my energies into doing the best job I could. Because if I could just be good at something, if I could just succeed in my job, as I was failing at getting pregnant, I might just feel better about myself. And so, that was exactly what I did. During my five hours at work, I once again repeated that self-sacrificing ritual I had become so accustomed to – not taking a lunch break, not eating or drinking much at all, not even taking bathroom breaks. It was incredible what I was depriving myself of for the sake of achieving in my job. I completely focused on my work, and in the meantime, my resentment and my sadness grew and grew.

It wasn't the job itself that I hated; I was so unhappy because I wasn't being true to myself – I wasn't in the right environment for my personality; I wasn't connected to my reality. With this job, and with every other office job I'd had before it, the same thing happened each time – I inevitably became desperately unhappy, no matter what type of office I worked in. But I never understood why, and so I always kept going back to more office jobs.

It was in this particular job as an Accounts Clerk, which in fact turned out to be my last office job, where I finally learned why I kept repeating this same pattern of working in a job that was just not suitable for me. This job was the one that would break a pattern I'd created years before, a pattern that was so ingrained in me that I had never previously been able to recognise it, or rectify it.

I got to a point where the stress finally caught up with me, and I got very sick. It was one and a half years into the job, and being so sick became the deciding factor in quitting work. I realised I had to stop and take time to heal, and just really focus on my health. And that meant taking all the stress out of my life – it meant I had to leave work altogether.

So I resigned, and from that moment on, I started to feel amazing. An overwhelming rush of freedom, a huge release of emotions, came over me. In fact, it was so intense that I lost ten kilos in just a couple of months after my resignation. The weight of pain, of resentment, of unhappiness, all the bingeing, just melted right off my body. I started to shine once more, and my inner light came back on.

It was then, after twelve years of working in an office environment, that I finally realised I just didn't belong in an office job at all. It didn't suit my creative, bubbly, and free-spirited personality. For so long, I was in and out of offices, always trying so hard to fit in, doing the best job I possibly could, but always feeling so alienated, so crushed, and finally always burning out and quitting – only to start the cycle again in the very next job! But no more, as I had finally learned, this was my 'working life' awakening. It took me getting very sick to wake me up and make me realise something had to change. Isn't it sad that it usually takes something drastic to make us stop and change our ways? So I finally broke the cycle, the pattern I had created for myself so long ago. This was the last office job I would ever have. I was now free to be me, to explore what I really wanted to do.

So many people remain stuck, just as I was, not knowing how to break the cycle, and very often, as was the case with me for such a long time, not actually realising that there is a problem at all. It's all too easy to remain sitting still in an unfulfilling comfort zone, only because it feels safe. And I'm not just talking about a work situation; it is so in relationships too.

You need guts, a sense of adventure, and dreams to chase, to be able to make a change in your life. You need to take calculated risks in order to set the wheels in motion, to re-start the machine that is your being, to evolve and get one step closer to your ultimate destination. And luckily, I have all of that. I have guts, a real sense of adventure, and I will always have dreams that I will never stop chasing.

The other very important reason why I left my job, of course, was to take that particular stress out of my life, so that I could focus only on getting pregnant. I had to remove as much stress from my life as I could, to give myself every possible chance of falling pregnant. It was the best thing I could have done. Leaving work gave me peace, rest, and freedom from a very restrictive and unhappy life. My infertility journey had begun long before my resignation, but now, after removing the stress of work from my life, I was finally able to focus on delving deeper into finding solutions to heal my body and my soul.

Since my infertility journey started, I had tried many different avenues to help me fall pregnant. There was the fertility clinic I had been in and out of for two years, and there was also Holistic Therapy, which was amazing in teaching me about myself, as well as removing blocks and fears from my mind. The therapies I used were Homeopathy, Kinesiology, Hypnotherapy, and Acupuncture. I never stopped trying to heal myself, trying to find out the reasons why I wasn't falling pregnant, and at the same time, trying to evolve into a better, healthier version of myself.

There were two main issues with my inability to fall pregnant. The first crucial issue was my physical health, which had suffered for so long due to my eating disorder. I didn't know how to cope with anything without bingeing on food. In fact I had lived with it for so long that it had become such a part of my life – such a part of me. I didn't know how to live without it, and I actually got to a point where I accepted it as normal. The other crucial issue I discovered through Kinesiology was that I was actually ridden with multiple fears about pregnancy, and, as a consequence, I had subconsciously created blocks in my mind, which were directly affecting my ability to fall pregnant.

The human brain is an amazing and very complex organ. It controls absolutely everything that makes us who we are, every thought we have, and every part of our body. It is capable of magic, but also of destruction. We each have the power to create and achieve absolutely anything we want. But our thoughts can also hinder our ability to function healthily, if our minds get stuck in a world of negativity. And this is where finding your true self comes in. Your true self is fearless, positive, magical, and beautiful. Your true self is actually able to control your mind and turn it around to come out of its thoughts of negativity, and instead bring back thoughts of positivity. But for that to happen, you need to listen to your true self; you need to listen, acknowledge, and honour the real you. And I, of course, wasn't doing this, hence the fears and the blocks about pregnancy.

It took six months of exploring different natural therapies to finally, after a seventeen year battle, regain control over my eating disorder. What drove me to this point was my desire to abolish every fear and block I had about pregnancy. The fears and blocks I had were all manifested in my mind, therefore, it was my mind that I had to work on. So I decided to try Hypnotherapy, which directly works on the subconscious mind, overriding the conscious mind – the mind that encourages negative thoughts. And interestingly, my decision to seek help with my pregnancy issues caused me to come face to face with my eating disorder, see it for what it really was, and regain control over it. This was how I was able to finally take back the power it had had over me for such a long time.

Ironically, I had begun my Hypnotherapy sessions to work on my issues about pregnancy, but when my eating disorder came up instead, it clearly became a priority to address that first, as I had to be physically healthy before I could work on becoming pregnant. It took only three sessions to completely change a way of life that I had grown to accept as normal. I have said already that we are magical beings, capable of achieving anything we want. I had just proven that to myself. It is not the therapists who fix your problems; they are merely a guide to help you get to your ultimate destination. *You* are actually the one who fixes your problems.

The only way Hypnotherapy will really work for you is if you truly want to change. I absolutely wanted to change. I hated my eating disorder with a passion, but I didn't know how to live without it. I wanted it gone, out of my life, never to return, but without it, I had no other coping mechanism to rely on.

My therapist and I started working on the reasons why it had all started in the first place, and from there everything just came out of me like an avalanche, unable to stop until I had confessed and addressed every feeling associated with the eating disorder – every feeling I had about myself. I became an open book, raw with emotion...

It was a very young Claire who I saw as the Binger – she binged to fill an empty space within her, she binged to fill herself with what she saw as comfort, love, and protection. In reality, this had begun when I was a teen, as a consequence of self-esteem issues at school. But in therapy, I didn't see the teen, I saw myself as a young child. There was also another person in this scenario – myself as a grown woman. And that Claire was the Punisher. She would punish young Claire for being weak, for disgracing herself by bingeing. She would punish her by making her purge, and then by starving her, until such time as young Claire would be so hungry that she would binge and start the cycle all over again.

And so the scene was set, and the cycle became apparent. The cycle began with not coping, followed by bingeing, and then finished with a cruel punishment – purging and starving. It was classic Bulimia. And contrary to popular belief, Bulimia is not about the food itself, but what the food does for the individual. Eating the food is merely a tool for coping. It could also easily be drugs, alcohol, and numerous other things that the individual uses as a coping mechanism – a crutch. But I used food. Bulimia is an addiction, a repetitive pattern, during which an individual associates food with taking the pain and the problems away. The food becomes the anaesthetic.

Having established the scene, we then began to integrate the two Claire's – the Binger and the Punisher, to make them understand each other, learn from each other, and finally work together to become one very strong unity. This counselling, along with affirmations spoken directly to my subconscious mind while under a peaceful trance, stopped the cycle, and put in place other healthy coping mechanisms, which finally gave me freedom from this hell I had lived with for so long. I was now one step closer to my goal of falling pregnant, as my body would finally begin its healing process to be better able to carry a child.

Having addressed the eating disorder, my Hypnotherapist and I were then able to start working on removing the fears and blocks I had about falling pregnant. Of course, the blocks had been created by the fears – the fear of gaining weight during my pregnancy, losing control over my body, the fear of labour, and the fear of the responsibility of being a mother, and the enormity that came with that responsibility. My fears were abundant.

In the gentle trances, I would see my child, a girl, and really connect with her, and feel at peace – a peace where all my fears would disappear, and I just felt love for my child. It was during these trances that I saw there was nothing to fear about pregnancy; I saw, in fact, that the reality of pregnancy was love and beauty. And, of course, the moment the fears disappeared, so did the blocks.

All in all, the process didn't take very long, and after a couple of months I felt stronger, and finally able to accept and receive my child.

After Hypnotherapy, I no longer felt I was pushing away the help available to me to become pregnant. Because you see, although I had tried various techniques to fall pregnant, and although I always believed that all my energies were completely focused on falling pregnant, I was in fact self-sabotaging the whole time. Without realising it, and certainly without meaning to, I was so afraid that subconsciously I was stopping and rejecting the process. I was fruitlessly charging ahead on the baby wagon going backwards. It took me two years to realise this.

My infertility journey may have been a painful and difficult phase in my life, but it was also an amazing learning experience, an immense evolvement. Would I have ever made the decision to tackle my eating disorder head on, if it hadn't been for my inability to fall pregnant? Perhaps not, but because of the infertility I did, and after therapy, I knew within my heart that from then on, I would always have the strength and the ability to fight and conquer my eating disorder, should it ever come back. Again, sometimes what *doesn't* glitter can turn into gold – my infertility caused me to understand, challenge, and conquer my eating disorder. There are blessings in disguise all around us...

I learned a lot during my infertility journey, one of the most important lessons being to accept the now – the now being my life in the present moment. Take a step back, and look at your life from a suspended point of view – as if you were looking down at yourself in your world. What do you see? You will be amazed at what you find. Begin with yourself, your health, and then continue to what surrounds you – your family and friends, your home, your job, and finally see all the little extras – like what you do on the weekends, the holidays you go on, even the car you drive. Amazing, isn't it? I mean, how lucky are you? You have so much!

The beauty of looking at your life for what it is in the now is that you will only see what you *do* have – you cannot see what isn't there, and therefore, you cannot see or miss what you *don't* have.

All too often, we focus more on what we don't have, as opposed to what we do have. But if we learn to accept and appreciate what we do have, more of the things we want but don't yet have will start to come into our lives. Without having to push and force, the things we want will gently, smoothly, and most often unexpectedly come into our lives. It is the power of attraction – positive attracts positive, and the same goes for negative.

Yes, we all want different things, and we always want more, so absolutely we must have goals and work towards them, but work towards them without expectations, because expectations create pressure, which in turn create stress and negativity. And of course, expectations are projections into the future – the future which hasn't happened yet and therefore isn't real.

True happiness is all about accepting our life for the now, all the while looking forward to the future without expectation, but instead with optimism and hope.

Expectations of our future also tip the scales, the scales being the perfect balance that is our life... For example, have you ever planned a big New Year's Eve party, only to find yourself not enjoying the night as much as you expected to? And, on the flipside, have you ever not bothered to organise anything at all for New Year's Eve, only to end up having the most wonderful night? This pattern had been apparent to me for a while, but I didn't quite understand why everything happened that way. I mean, what was the point in looking forward to anything, or getting excited about anything, if the outcome was going to be the complete opposite of my high expectations? Did this then mean that to get a positive result, I had to expect the worst? Hence the scales of life – two extremes, high and low. If we keep tipping the scales one way or the other, our life will not be balanced. Without expectations, we are less likely to experience such extremes, and therefore keep in that even keel, and stay in that perfect balance.

It was a girlfriend who gave me my answer. Through her learning of Yoga, she had been made aware of perfect balance in every aspect of life. As she explained this to me, all of a sudden it made sense! All highs are balanced with a subsequent low, and vice versa. Life never remains in either extreme for long, before it is balanced in the opposite direction, to get back to that perfect balance. What an amazing awakening! Understanding this made such a difference to my life. It's about taking the steps to reach your goals, but not having expectations and trying to control the outcome. It's about accepting the here and now, and not focusing on what we don't have. It's about enjoying life in the moment, all the while believing in, and working towards our dreams.

And so, I applied this profoundly rejuvenating, yet very balanced, way of living to my life. The release of pressure I felt was incredible. No expectations, therefore no pressure or stress, just a constant, balanced evolvement of self.

For over two years, each and every month, I had expectations. I absolutely had to be pregnant, or my world would fall apart. And sure enough, every single month my world did fall apart. I crumbled into a million pieces of sadness, anger and helplessness, as I constantly faced negative pregnancy tests.

The fact was I just couldn't control the future, though I desperately tried to, despite the continual disappointments. But I never had any control over the outcome. No matter how hard I tried, no matter what I did, I couldn't change the outcome; it was going to be what it was going to be.

I remember all the days of hoping, of wishing, of wanting so badly for that little pink line to appear on the pregnancy test – for my positive result. But it never came. All my focus was on what I didn't have, and I just couldn't see what I did have – how rich my life already was. All I could see was that I still wasn't pregnant.

I had yet another awakening around my 33$^{rd}$ birthday. For a number of reasons, my husband and I made the decision to change our fertility specialist, and consequently our new doctor changed everything. Very aggressive and factual in his manner, he confronted us with a few heavy medical truths.

To begin with, I had a very low ovarian reserve, and on top of that, the few eggs that I did have weren't maturing properly. Added to this was the shock of learning that I also had Endometriosis. All this very upsetting news brought in a realisation that we may not even be able to have children at all. My husband and I were devastated and absolutely heartbroken. We felt as though our whole world had fallen apart. But even though I felt completely crushed, after getting past the initial shock, I realised what we had to do, and jumped into gear straight away – my optimism shining through again.

What we had to do was *accept* – accept the life we had, and appreciate all the wonderful things that surrounded us. And so what I began to see again, after two and a half years of blindness, was the most beautiful and privileged life. We had so much! We actually had the most amazing life together – from our families and friends, our adorable little dog, to our lifestyle, and finally and most importantly, to each other. The bond my husband and I share is founded on deep love and a strong commitment to each other. It is an amazing bond that keeps on growing each and every single day. We are so blessed to have each other, to be as one for the rest of our lives.

I saw, for the first time in a long time, my life for what it really was. I saw true beauty, I saw magic, and then suddenly, I was completely fulfilled; I didn't need anything else to be happy; I didn't need to be pregnant.

For a long time, I couldn't see past being a mother. For a long time, I felt that if I couldn't be a mother, there would be nothing else for me. I felt I had no other purpose in life. I was so wrong. I was completely blind to who I was, what I had, and what I could actually do with my life.

Every month was completely dedicated to getting pregnant. There was nothing else. So imagine the devastation of not being pregnant every single month; imagine the slap in the face, over, and over again. Imagine the feeling of failure, of defeat, and of shame. Shame was a dominant emotion throughout my infertility journey. I felt shame every day. I felt shame around my family and friends, especially my friends. Our friends started to fall pregnant from the moment we got married – from the moment we started trying to fall pregnant ourselves. One by one, all around us, everyone was falling pregnant. And although each time I was able to share in my friends' happiness, each time also felt like a stab in the heart for me. I couldn't understand why it was so easy for them. There wasn't a single other couple in our circle of friends who had any fertility problems at all. Just us, just me! And so, as more and more of our friends fell pregnant around us, the more I fell into a hole of complete and utter shame and embarrassment. I wanted them to stop; I wanted to stop hearing that people were falling pregnant. I couldn't separate myself from the darkness of failure overtaking me.

After a while though, they did stop falling pregnant, and I felt strength slowly creep back into my soul, for a little while anyway, because before I knew it, round two had begun. Our friends were having their second child! However, this time, before I began to fall back into that deep, dark hole of shame, I suddenly realised what I was putting myself through. I was focusing on everyone else's life rather than my own! I was again denying myself love and acceptance. I was focusing on what I didn't have, and I was completely blinded by the embarrassment and the heartbreak I was feeling. I couldn't see the beauty of my own world. So I started to very carefully pull the situation apart – why wasn't I falling pregnant? I wanted to get to the bottom of what was really going on. I began to focus on myself, instead of others.

It is in human nature to follow, to want what someone else has, to not feel satisfied until we are like everybody else. But the reality is that we are actually all so different, beginning simply with the way we look. We are all physically so unique – even identical twins are not one hundred per cent identical. And it's as simple as that; that's all we really need to understand to make us realise that we can't actually be like anybody else anyway. Each and every one of us is a uniquely created being, with a uniquely different story from that of the next human being. We all have our own story, our own life path, and no one else has the same story, or life path. Therefore, it's actually impossible to be like everybody else.

I applied this way of thinking to my situation. All our friends around us: it didn't actually matter whether they were pregnant or not, whether they had babies or not, because it was their story, and not ours. Their story had absolutely nothing to do with ours. We had our own story, our own different and beautiful story, unlike anyone else's. This helped me immensely not only in my infertility journey, but in so many aspects of my life.

Once again, I felt a burst of freedom that just rushed in and released the pressure of turmoil that was suffocating me. I was then able to rebuild my inner strength, my faith in myself, and my overall confidence. I was then able to let the real Claire, the real me, shine through again, knowing I was unique, with my own wonderful, beautiful story; knowing that I didn't have to be pregnant to be special.

And so, as you can see, through my painful journey, I actually accomplished many amazing things. I had life changing awakenings that taught me to view things from a different perspective; I was able to see my life for what it really was, rich with beauty, and I was able to let go of missing the things I wanted but didn't yet have. I began to work towards attaining the things I wanted with determination and vigour, but of course, without expectation. I learned that we can all ultimately get what we truly desire, and that nothing is impossible. And I learned that we are all unique and magical beings, each with our own beauty, and our own story.

But I also learned how fragile we can be, and how easy it is to hurt ourselves and others around us, simply by being blind to positivity, and instead suffocate ourselves with negativity.

Finally, I learned that we never sit still, as we are constantly moving – either evolving, or dissolving. We are all part of life's perfect balance, life's perfect scales. Life is actually very simple; it's not hard to break down a problem and find a solution. It's not difficult to find your way if you listen to your true self.

I was only 33 years old, and I had already seen and accomplished so much in my life, but I also still had so many wonderful adventures ahead of me, as well as gruelling battles to fight, and happy victories to celebrate . . . Victories such as this one, this miracle, the greatest victory of my life...

### We got pregnant!! ☺

Yes, we did it! After over two and a half years of hard work, of tears, of dedication, our dream had finally come true!

The way I felt when I saw those two little pink lines was indescribable. A miracle, a blessing, had been bestowed upon my husband and me. We couldn't have been more overjoyed and excited about the incredible gift we were to receive the following year.

The journey we had to take to bring us to this point was life changing, and though sometimes heartbreaking, because we had each other, our love pulled us through.

The strength and the love my husband and I had together was what kept us going; it was what kept us together through the difficult times, and it is what will hold us together as one for the rest of our lives.

However, there is another factor to this happy ending, and I will now tell you how it finally happened, how we finally got pregnant. I will now tell you the turning point in our journey, what threw us in the deep end, but also made our dream come true...

It is important to recognise patterns, and how easy it is to stay within them. Being stuck in patterns can be like Groundhog Day – the same thing over and over, either rolling along comfortably, or making the same mistakes repeatedly, but never actually evolving anywhere. And these repetitive patterns can be applied to any part of our lives, including work, health, or relationships.

I have spoken about the work pattern I created for myself, remaining in unfulfilling jobs, and I have also spoken of the health pattern I remained stuck in for such a big part of my life, my eating disorder. But I had a relationship pattern as well, which I broke out of through my relationship with my husband. This particular relationship pattern was directly linked to my fear of commitment, of responsibility, and subsequently, this pattern affected my infertility journey, as having a child, in my mind, was one of the biggest responsibilities I could ever face.

Actually, this kind of relationship pattern is really not uncommon; it's fear based – fear of the future, fear of the unknown, fear of failure, and most importantly for me, it was fear of commitment, fear of losing my freedom. It was an unbelievable fear of responsibility.

For years, I jumped from one relationship to the next, my record relationship lasting no longer than two years. I was stuck in this pattern of honeymoon period, then settling down and getting comfortable, and finally boredom, and leaving the relationship. I wasn't able to take it to the next level; I wasn't able to go deeper and accept the responsibility that came with a serious, long lasting commitment. I feared the responsibility, and so I ran away. And each time I left a relationship, I felt so free and liberated, I felt so alive, but before long I would repeat the cycle again with the next guy. And it wouldn't be long between relationships either; I can safely say that I am not at all familiar with the single life, but that's ok, because I have never been a girl who enjoys being alone.

In any case, despite always being involved with someone, I was still able to do all the things I wanted to do. My freedom in that sense was never affected. I cannot say I missed out on anything in my life just because I was always involved with someone. It wasn't freedom from day to day activities that I felt I was missing out on by being in a committed relationship; it was freedom from reality, reality being responsibility.

This massive fear of responsibility I carried with me was absolutely one of the reasons why I left a very significant relationship in my life. Along with trying to cope with my eating disorder, which was destroying who I was, I also crumbled under the pressure to marry this man, and to never have the freedom to have other experiences. I associated marriage with being trapped, with limitations on my life. I couldn't have been more wrong.

And so I ran away. I ran away from the responsibility of committing myself fully to the one man. But in this case I wasn't just running away from responsibility; there were also the demons I was battling with – my eating disorder, as well as a lack of compatibility between my partner and me, a compatibility that is vital to any relationship's survival; we were too different.

Hence I didn't make the decision to leave this relationship only because of my fear of responsibility; there were actually other factors involved as well. I say this because leaving this relationship was the right thing to do, albeit my fear of responsibility being one of the reasons.

Many of us, however, leave relationships for reasons purely based on this fear of responsibility, this fear of commitment. And with so much temptation around us, it can be all too easy to succumb to escaping our reality, and leave a relationship the moment it starts to get serious. So there lay my relationship pattern, my fear of responsibility, and this was a direct connection to my infertility journey.

Having a baby, for me, was one of the biggest, most important, life changing responsibilities I could ever face in my life. And my battle here was to end the fight between wanting a baby so badly, and being scared to death of the responsibility of both carrying that child, and being his/her parent. What a battle! Of course, I didn't realise there actually was a battle to conquer at all, until I started having Kinesiology sessions, where I discovered that I was suppressing a multitude of emotions, amongst them feelings of intense fear. In fact, I was suppressing so much that it was affecting me physically, and completely hindering my chances of falling pregnant. I was unconsciously self-sabotaging. My conscious mind wanted the baby, but my unconscious mind feared the baby, and everything that came with it. Very often what the conscious mind and the unconscious mind are both thinking can be vastly different. A healthy mind is forming a connection between the two, creating an understanding, and finding balance.

Well, I did find balance – through a number of holistic therapies, and through writing. Each of these healing techniques, in their own unique way, helped me to understand what I was feeling, and most importantly, what was real. And that was when I learned that my fears were in fact not real. Fears are merely a figment of our imagination, a passing thought, manifested from all that we see, and all that we hear around us. Fears are projections into the future – the future that hasn't yet happened, and therefore does not exist, as the future is unknown, and is always subject to change. Fear is a waste of our precious emotions, hindering our lives in the most negative way.

Understanding this made everything so much clearer for me. There was such relief, such freedom, and a clearing of the path to my future, all of which enabled me to really see and accept what was, and not be afraid of what was to come. This was when I started to stop fearing the future, and accept the life I had with my husband, and this was also the very moment that I started to *receive* very quickly.

No sooner had I started to accept my life as it was, with all its richness, suddenly the wheels of the machine that is life began to turn aggressively, taking me to unknown, frightening, but also very exciting territory...

After accepting our life as it was without a baby, it only took one month to actually fall pregnant! But that one month was one of the most confronting, challenging, but exciting months of my life. The speed at which everything started to fall into place and perfectly align was astounding – within that one month, where I had come to accept my life in the now, where I had left all my fears behind, everything changed. We were on a rollercoaster to success, with no turning back.

Rewinding back to my 33$^{rd}$ birthday, having made the decision to change to this amazingly talented fertility specialist immediately threw us in the deep end. The tests, the appointments, the medical inductions, the countless needles; a crescendo of emotional upheavals took over our world. We were in shock, and completely overwhelmed, but at the same time it was dynamic and exciting, as we could feel we had been thrust into this amazing adventure for a reason. Deep down, we both knew this would ultimately take us to the destination we had waited so long to get to.

There was something else, something beautiful, something pure that also helped to get us pregnant; it was a belief in a higher being – a belief in angels. I haven't believed solely in my dreams to get me through life; I have also believed in angels – Guardian Angels, angels who guide and protect me, and who are always with me, no matter where, no matter what.

Many times throughout my life I have experienced very low points, but not once have I actually gone so far as to hit rock-bottom. How? Because my angels are always with me, protecting and guiding me…

Now you can choose to believe or not, but they are there, all around us, if only you could listen, if only you could feel their presence and know that you're never alone, but always protected. Your intuition, that inner voice that doesn't need to think, that voice in your subconscious that always guides you in the right direction, *that* is actually the voice of your Guardian Angels. Your 'gut feeling': that is your angels. It's a beautiful feeling knowing you're never alone, knowing that no matter where you are in your life, your Guardian Angels are always with you. Believing in my angels and listening to them is also what helped me get to my ultimate destination. It is what kept me going, what kept me positive throughout my whole infertility journey, and what instinctively made me know deep down that everything was going to be alright. My angels were, and are, my faith.

Listening to the messages my angels send me, and asking them for guidance, has helped me immensely, with every aspect of my life. Believing in angels is basically a core belief in the good of all things around us. It's that warm, fuzzy feeling inside you that makes you feel safe and secure. And sometimes, when you have that bad feeling in the pit of your stomach, that is also your angels – your intuition letting you know something is wrong. It is always there, that inner voice, your angels protecting and guiding you, in whichever way you need at the time. It is a belief and a trust in yourself, your true self, and it fills your whole being with a bright, shiny light, with positivity.

Another very important factor that helped to bring us our miracle was our absolute commitment and hard-working approach to the task. From the moment we changed fertility specialist, it was full on – jumping in, getting out of our comfort zone, taking a risk, and facing our fears and the challenge head on. Not that the previous two and a half years of trying to get pregnant wasn't a huge emotional effort, but this particular chapter was very aggressive, very quick, and full force. It had to be this way, as after hearing our specialist's medical opinion, we knew we had to act fast – there wasn't much time on our side.

This change was like an explosion in my husband's and my life. We immediately dedicated all our time to appointments set before the sun even rose in the morning; we were given multiple and intrusive tests, inductions into the IVF world, and I was confined within very strict timetables to both prepare, and administer all the injections of fertility drugs myself.

It was overwhelming, but it was this dedicated approach, combined with releasing all my fears, accepting the now, and listening to my angels, that enabled my husband and me to finally reach the pot of gold at the end of our rainbow, the end of our incredible infertility journey.

It was mid August 2010 when those two little pink lines appeared on the pregnancy test. We were two weeks away from going through with IVF, when we miraculously fell pregnant with an IUI (Intra Uterine Insemination) – a medical procedure where the sperm is injected into the cervix, which is a lot less intrusive than IVF, and I might add, a lot less expensive.

My life was so full, so rich, and the more I saw this, the more I focused on all the goodness surrounding me, the more quickly I received amazing, beautiful gifts. I truly believe that the IUI was successful because of this.

We were amazed, we were overjoyed, we were blessed; we were finally pregnant! ☺

I had conquered again in my life. And with all that I learned and discovered about myself and life through this journey, I was so much better equipped for my future than ever before. The world was my oyster, and everything ahead of me looked bright.

Of course, I knew there would be more challenges and battles to fight along the way, as such is life, but with the incredible feeling of power, and the fire and determination inside me, there wasn't anything I couldn't face and conquer from then onwards.

I had been on a very powerful journey of self-discovery. I had found, reconnected with, and accepted the real Claire. I had grown and evolved into my true self. I know who I am now, and more importantly, I love who I am. However, I have certainly not finished learning, growing, and evolving, as that is the unfinished road of life ahead of me – a never ending road that enables each of us to reach for the stars, and never ever have limitations.

I know there will no doubt be more setbacks throughout my life; an eating disorder doesn't disappear overnight, and self-esteem can be fragile and easily disturbed. But with all that I learned from my incredible journey, I knew I would challenge each setback with strength, determination, and pride.

So dream your dreams, believe in them, and work hard to make them come true. Listen to your angels, and trust in your inner voice. Be your true self, let your inner light shine bright, love the beautiful soul you are, and pamper the amazing vessel that is your body – the miraculous being that carries you through the journey of life.

Look around you, at everything you have, see how rich you really are, revel in your abundance, and see how quickly your world begins to fill up with more goodness, positivity, and all the things your dreams are made of.

Life is amazing, so wondrously beautiful. I have opened my heart and shown you a part of my world; I have shown you that nothing is impossible, that there are no limitations, and no endings. With love and determination, you will get absolutely anything your heart desires.

By being your true self, you can attain your perfect life. Create your adventures, meet your challenges and strive to realise your dreams, for you have the infinite power to control absolutely everything that enters your world. And if you fall back at times, that's ok too, as it's merely another opportunity for you to evolve even more. One cannot learn without setbacks – setbacks force us to push, to fight. Setbacks are actually little blessings in disguise. As long as we keep learning, evolving, always moving forward, and most importantly, enjoying our blessed lives, and loving our beautiful selves, almost anything is possible.

As I saw my baby move for the first time, its little arms and legs, a tiny little being living and growing inside of me, I was again reminded of the true miracle of life – such beauty, such magical wonderment.

And as I ride the relentless waves of life's ups and downs with my loving husband by my side, I am calm, I am strong and positive, and I am so excited about all the possibilities, all the amazing things I am yet to experience.

I have created the amazing life I live today, and my future looks so bright, as I am bringing with me the wisdom I have gradually acquired, the strength and courage I have developed and, most importantly, the love and respect I now have for myself. I now feel able to conquer anything that comes my way, and that paves an exciting road for my future.

Through my eyes you have seen into a part of my world, some of my battles, some of my achievements; through my eyes I have shown you a chapter of my journey through life's many adventures.

I was a little girl lost, that bloomed into an incredibly strong and self-assured woman.

I finish this journey with you in a beautiful place, with an abundance of love, strength, and determination, with an open heart to the beauty and goodness of this world, an infinite well of positivity, possibility and magic, a place where absolutely anyone can reside, and bask in its exuberantly bright, shiny light…

*Power, strength, determination, fight*
*Magic, abundance, clarity, acceptance*
*Love and light, to your perfect life* ♥

by
Claire Howard

## About Claire Howard

Claire was born in France in 1977, and migrated to Australia with her parents and her sister in 1986. She is bilingual in both French and English.

Claire lives in Brisbane with her husband and two children, and fills her life with looking after her family.

After leaving an unfulfilling life as an Admin Office worker, Claire took to writing, and composed her first book, Through My Eyes, which is about various challenges she has faced in her life and how she has overcome them.

Claire writes to share her stories in the hope of helping others facing similar challenges to overcome theirs, and realise their true potential, their true love, whilst living a positive life.

She is a free spirit who lives her life optimistically, always looking for the positive and the beauty in everything, and she is passionate about finding and learning new ways to self-heal in both the spiritual, and the natural world.

Claire is living her dream, having created the family she has always desired, and writing from her heart to help others live their perfect life.

 www.facebook.com/xclairehowardx

# Soul Sista Jess

### Written by Jess Welsh

I've been told that from the moment of birth, I was quite a text book baby. My very early years were quite simple. I lived with my mum and dad and my older sister, who was 7 when I was born, would come to stay with us often and visit. My mum worked in the knitting mill and my dad was a slaughter man at the local abattoir. Once I started walking, the mischief began. There were a few moments from my younger years that I have recollections of to this day. One of my favourites is remembering back to being a little younger than 18 months old. My mum and I were out the back and mum went inside briefly, only to return and notice that I had disappeared. I can't recall why and I don't remember going through the fence but I do remember looking down the giant rock wall and encouraging our dog Judy the Jack Russell to follow me. I proceeded to slide down on my little bum into the drain. I remember looking each way and deciding to go to the left. There was very little water in the drain and I remember it being quite a warm day. Judy and I headed to the left and walked through the dark tunnel which was of course the drain going under a main road. Over the other side of the tunnel was the local park which had a large pond and always had ducks swimming, and playing around. I wandered along for a while and then realized I didn't want to be down there; I wanted to go home. Judy and I headed back and came to the tunnel again, although this time it scared me. I didn't want to walk through it again. I'm unsure if it was the noise of the cars or something else but nothing had bothered me about it the first time. I stood there crying and scared for only a few moments before my mum came running to me. She picked me up and held me so tight. I can remember my mum holding me and walking back towards the local park to get us out and fortunately there was a man close by to the drain who helped to get mum, Judy and me out. From that moment on I knew that my mum was always going to do whatever she could to help me; she was after all my very own guardian angel here on earth.

When I reached 18 months old my mum and dad split up and at around the age of two we moved in to my mum's boyfriend's house. He was a truck driver who often drove interstate so that we didn't see him a great deal. A couple of months after turning three I got my first sibling, my baby brother Garrett. I don't remember a lot about Garrett when he was a baby but I do know how proud I was to have him! Another few years later, after I had started primary school, I was given yet another baby brother Tristian. I can remember begging mum one morning to come into the classroom with him so that I could show him off to everybody for show and tell so that the class could see just how lucky I was to have two brothers. By the time I reached the age of 7 I had a little sister Chanel. I can remember her in her pretty white nightie and thinking just how cute she was. I was so excited to walk out of school that afternoon and see that Peter's friend was there to pick me up, knowing that I would soon have another baby to love.

My mum was a very busy lady with four children to raise. At about the age of six my step dad had left truck driving to work locally so that he could spend more time with his family and really get to know his children. My mum and step dad got married; it was quite a basic and simple ceremony held at our house with only very few family members to witness their union.

One day, when I was three, my mum heard a little girl next door and asked her if she would like to come over and have a play with me. Her name was Sally; she was the same age as I was and little did we know that this would be a long term friendship. I used to get so excited when I saw her mum's car pull up next door.

Garrett and I used to play around quite a lot. We would often be found riding our push bikes through the bush across the road and riding through puddles and coming home covered in mud and making mum see red when we trounced it through her clean house. We had so much fun riding for hours on end but between the good times Garrett and I did have some bad times. He had a temper just like his dad and on several occasions I had done something to egg him into what seemed like a psychotic outburst. One in particular was when he was riding his push bike over a jump in the bush and I decided to throw a rock at him which hit him on the corner of his left eyebrow. He didn't end up going into a fit of rage, he instead rode off crying and I knew instantly that I was going to be in so much trouble. It wasn't long before I could see my step dad storming my way and I could've sworn that I could see steam pouring from his ears. To top it off there were also many occasions where I had never done anything to Garrett to set him off either yet I still got the blame. Perhaps a bit of karma for my previous efforts!

I did a few extracurricular activities when I was younger but none lasted very long because I was more interested in being a social butterfly. At school I had few friends but they often chopped and changed because of falling out and differences of opinion. My mum was always asking me to find better friends, instead of friends that were nasty and mean at times. Right from a young age my mum has always wanted the best for me and I never saw it that way; I used to think that she just wanted to tell me what to do. For as long as I can remember I've always been extremely stubborn, headstrong and determined. I liked to do things myself and "had" to do it once I put my mind to it as well as doing it in my own way. This often caused issues between my mum and me and especially between myself and my step dad. I can recall thinking on numerous occasions, "who is he to tell me what to do? He's not my dad!" If only I had known what I now know! I found a new outlet in music and even began taking my Walkman to school with me. I threw myself into listening to music and as I grew older it became a concern of my mum's. I could understand why but I enjoyed it so much and would spend hours with it turned up. Singing and dancing had become my release over the years.

My dad lived with his girlfriend Maree who had a daughter 6 years my senior and for the most part we got along well. They lived about ten minutes out of town in a renovated old barn that had two stories. I thought this place was great. There was a bit of land at the back of the house, and there was a chook pen. I used to take the scraps out to the chooks and lock them up and collect the eggs when I would let them out in the morning. I used to love going out there until they got a rooster. He was a nasty thing who still had his spurs and wasn't just a regular rooster. He was a special breed who liked to chase you and stir you up. Maree even had to take the broom to the clothes line with her in case he decided to sneak up. Way down the back paddock was a dam and there was also a dam in the paddock to the right of the barn and was quite close to the fence. We would occasionally go over and spend the day with some diced meat and cotton catching yabbies. I convinced dad to make me a "catcher" because there was no way I was touching the yabbies to pull them out of the dam. I had spent quite a lot of time at the dams skimming rocks and looking for frogs. Occasionally my older sister would come out and stay in dad's caravan beside the barn, but she was much older than me and had a part time job and a social life to maintain.

I can recall one Friday afternoon when my dad came to pick me up. It was the school holidays at the beginning of my final year at primary school. He told me that my nana George (her real name was Phyllis, but she used to walk around whistling Georgie girl often and George stuck) had had a stroke and was in hospital. He said she was quite sick and was probably going to die. My dad isn't a very emotional person and certainly doesn't like to express his emotions much like myself. I asked him if he could please take me to see her but he said that she was too sick and wouldn't know who I was. We went to his house and I knew it wasn't going to be a good outcome. I was ten years old and had never known anyone who was dying and had never dealt with a death before. I went to bed and spent quite some time lying there thinking of what I had seen in movies when someone died and just how sad everyone was and wondering if that's how I was going to feel. It was quite late and I heard the phone ring. I ran to the railing on the stairs and looked down because I could see all of the kitchen, lounge and dining room from there. I can't remember the words that my dad spoke to Maree once he hung up the phone but I knew instantly that my nana George was gone forever. I lay in bed for hours after that thinking about this sweet little lady who would get me a glass of orange soft drink and two juicy fruit chews that she kept in her fridge in an old pill container, whenever I would go and visit. I used to ride to her house on the school holidays and on weekends when I was bored to go and see her. She always found the time to talk to me and I always listened intently. I was no longer going to be able to do this, and I was shattered. I knew I would miss her dearly, but death was still a new concept for me and very difficult to understand fully at the age of ten.

My dad was nervous but quick to tell me the next morning that she had passed after suffering another two strokes. He told me that she didn't suffer and I was relieved to know that. I was upset the most by the sadness I could see in my dad's eyes. He would never say how he felt but I knew she meant the world to him. On many occasions throughout his life, my dad had lived with nana George and they had a great bond. She was the go to lady if you needed an item of clothing mended or a button sewn back on. When I went home we told mum about nana George's death and that dad would let me know when the funeral was if I wanted to go.

Mum and I had a talk about the funeral and she told me that I didn't have to go if I didn't want to. I told her that I needed to go. I wasn't able to go to the hospital to say goodbye and this was my only chance. I remember pulling up outside the chapel with my dad and once inside trying to work out all the faces that were there. I cried a little during the service and had some lavender with me that my mum and I picked out of her garden. We went to the afternoon tea afterwards and then dad dropped me home. I remember going to my room and writing in my diary what I had seen. I wrote the date, her name and a brief message for her. Over the next few weeks I would look in my diary and cry for short periods of time but once school resumed for the New Year I was distracted.

As I carried on through school, issues with friends had always continued and so did my changes in friends. I had made some friends in grade 6 that were so great and we got along so well. Birthday parties and hanging out in general were all a blast with my new friends, until the end of the year which approached very quickly. My friends Kimberley, Carrie and I went to the pool together one weekend and were having fun in the sun and playing in the water and all the while I was a little distracted about the thought of leaving them all behind to move over the road (literally) to high school. I ran up to do a bomb into the water and on my way down got Kim on the shoulder as she was climbing out, and knocked her back into the water. That was the end of that friendship. No matter what way or how many times I said sorry, it didn't count for anything. I grabbed my belongings and headed for home.

I started high school and made some new friends. We all got along well except getting the feeling that I was more of a "fourth" wheel, so to speak. This became apparent when I had my hair cut short for something different and one of the other girls picked on me and made it very clear that she thought I was copying her. I always felt a bit older than I actually was and couldn't understand why others had to be so childish, but the childishness continued when they got a lot of other people to make nasty comments to me and this was the beginning of being bullied. I tried my best to ignore it and get on with what I was doing. I became friends with a girl named Anne and we got on like a house on fire. We were both born under the zodiac sign of Aries and wanted to have fun. We didn't want to be held down; our school work did enough of that. We were often getting each other into a bit of strife at school and out of school but she didn't give a damn, so why shouldn't I? No one really seemed to care other than my family...but I didn't think that counted for much, after all it was their job...they would always be there. I used to clash with a lot of people in high school; I didn't know who I was and would often find that I hid the real me and was someone a little different. I took on a lot of the opinions and traits of my friends because it worked for them; why couldn't it work for me? Then I would find myself struggling and letting go of these attributes and being told by my friends that I had changed...I hadn't changed; I just stopped being someone I was not, yet this seemed to continue for a while.

Mel and I continued being friends through high school, as did Sally and I as we were at the same school now although she had her own friends from primary school that she hung around with. I would always say hi to her when I saw her but I did notice at times that when I did, it seemed as if she was ashamed to even respond to me or have been associated with me. I didn't really care; I guess that being like my dad and not really showing emotions had its benefits because I just kept on going. I would stew over things and brood but never talked about it with anyone; they were my thoughts and who would really want to know them?

My friend Kimberley from primary school had moved away with her family while I was mid-way through year seven and at the start of year ten her family moved back and she was returning to school with me. Although we saw each other around the school, we still didn't speak to each other and this at times upset me. Not wanting that to get me down, I forgot about it and moved on. About midyear, our entire school learnt of a fatal car accident in the early hours of that morning that tragically took Kim's life. She was with her boyfriend and a friend of his (who is also my cousin). They had been drinking and her boyfriend Billy wanted to drive. He was showing off and lost control and the final impact was with a power pole. Kim apparently died instantly. Billy and Leigh survived. My cousin Leigh had extensive leg damage and spent years having surgeries trying to correct the damage. He had a promising career ahead of himself as a motorbike racer, and that was gone forever in an instant. He has now had his lower leg amputated and has since got back on and ridden a motorbike! Billy ended up with a jail sentence and has always been terribly remorseful for his very silly actions, and this is something he will have to live with for the rest of his life. When I heard the news I didn't know what to think. She was a good friend to me previously, and how I wished we were able to have fixed things! I felt lost and found excuses during classes that day to go for walks and clear my head. I didn't attend her funeral. I heard it was a beautiful send off, but didn't feel that I deserved to be there. I often think about the pain that her family would still be feeling, and only hope that they have now come to peace with her sudden passing. Such a promising life taken too soon!

Sally and I became very on and off friends once we reached year nine which began at a different campus than where year 7 and 8 were studied. I had begun skipping school and was caught red handed one day by my own mum because silly me forgot it was her shopping day. My mum was at her wit's end with me and I moved in with my dad. Life was ok living with my dad. He and Maree had decided to live in separate houses a year or so after they had moved into town but after a while dad and Maree decided we should move back into the house (again for my dad anyway).

I was fourteen years old and thought I knew everything. I would go and visit my mum, my step dad and siblings but due to my step dad's work he often wasn't there as he was working late or doing overtime for extra income for his family. I had noticed that my step dad was being very "cool" with me. I don't think he was very impressed with me moving into my dad's and how I had been behaving, so there was always some tension there between us. I can now see why my step dad was upset by my moving out; he did after all spend a long time raising me as his own and supporting me. In 2001, while I was on a massive fad about the well-known band KISS, I saw an ad on TV that they were coming to Melbourne and asked him to take me. I asked as a joke but weeks later when he produced two tickets for us to go I was in shock. I couldn't believe it. We were going to see KISS, Live! I was so excited and was really surprised by this as we had always had a turbulent relationship. I was nervous about spending all that time with him alone purely because it was awkward. I didn't know what to say but all I knew is that he saved up and bought us tickets to see this band and it was our time to bond. It was great. There was a couple who were married on stage before the show. The screaming jets were the front band and once KISS came on stage it was bliss, except for one issue…I still cannot remember a lot of their performance! I've put it down to the excitement of the night.

Around the start of October 2003 my step dad and I had had a fight and the last words I said to him that day were, "I hate you, you're not my dad." His birthday was on the $17^{th}$ of October. He turned 42 and wasn't home when I went to visit, and at that time I was thankful. I was ashamed of what I had said to him; it was nasty and uncalled for but I justified it by putting it down to being a hormonal know it all teenager. I wrote him a note wishing him a happy birthday. I can recall seeing him on my walk to school one morning; he was driving out to work and he waved to me. I thought that was a good sign and that the storm was passing, slowly but surely anyway. On Thursday the 28th of November I was lying in bed early in the morning dreading getting up to get ready for yet another boring day of school. As I lay there thinking, I heard the phone ring.

I thought it was odd that the phone was ringing so early; it was only around 7:30am. I couldn't hear the conversation but my dad hung the phone up and walked down the hallway and into his and Maree's room which was next door to mine. The next thing I knew both dad and Maree were standing in my room. I looked at them and had a terrible feeling instantly. My dad's exact words were, "There's been an accident, Peter's dead. Your mum just rang and wants me to take you up to her house." At that very instant my terrible feeling was confirmed. I couldn't believe it. Dad and Maree left my room to give me some space. I didn't cry; I was trying to make sense of it. I kept thinking how? How could he have died? Maybe he took another short truck driving gig for some extra money and had an accident in the truck? That was the only thing I could think of that would've caused such a thing. I kept thinking of my brothers and sister and how they no longer had a dad and felt guilty because I still did. I thought of my mum and how much her heart would be breaking. Eventually I gave in and cried. I realised that it was my second last day of school and if I didn't go to school to hand in my work and do whatever work had to be done I wouldn't be going up into year 11. I had a freak out; it was almost like a panic attack and a defence mechanism due to the shock of what I was just told. I had to go to school, I had to.

Dad and Maree convinced me to stay home from school for the day and dad suggested that after we went up to mum's we would go into the school and talk to the principal. I felt sick the moment we pulled up out the front of my mum's house. I eased myself out of the car and slowly walked to the door with my dad. I didn't know how to deal with this. I am certainly no good at comforting people when they're upset; what was I going to do? I like to do good things; I like to help people and in this situation there was nothing I could do to help or make it any better, so I shut down. My mum came out the door to meet us and gave me such a big hug. I could immediately feel her pain oozing off her and it saddened me that she had to experience this, and that again there was nothing I could do. She lost her husband and would never see him again. She asked me to spend the day with them but I refused. I couldn't do it, and deep down I was disappointed with myself because I felt she needed me and I let her down. We went inside and the image of my brothers and sister sitting on the couch, eyes wide open and with no expressions on their faces, will always haunt me. They were so blank and I knew I could never take their pain away either. If I had the power to, I would've taken all the pain away from each of them, including my mum's even if it meant that it all went to me. No one deserves to feel that pain or sorrow and what did they ever do to deserve it? On the other hand, I was certain that I deserved it. We left and dad and I went to my school and spoke to my principal Mr. Hannan. I felt like some sort of science experiment or something odd, because it felt as though everyone was watching me and I could feel the sympathy coming from them from a mile away. I didn't want their sympathy. I didn't deserve anything; after all I was very quick to remind him that he wasn't my dad, so I deserved nothing.

The teachers and principal said they didn't care about my work and that I should take as much time off as I needed. This was a relief and one less thing for me to worry about. I asked dad if he could wait in the car park for ten minutes while I went around to my friends and told them why I wasn't going to be there. As soon as I got onto the oval Sally came running to me. She had stayed at her Nan's the night before and saw the police car early that morning and asked me what was happening. Sally and I hadn't really spoken in the past week but I was in no state to be bitter towards her, so I filled her in and she gave me a big hug. It seemed to be just what I needed at that time. She could sympathise with me to a certain degree as she was quite rebellious and stubborn as I was, especially towards her own step dad. We walked together up to where the rest of our friends were and I told them briefly what had happened and that I wouldn't be at school that day. They didn't know what to say and asked what happened; all I could say was that I didn't know. I left and dad and I went home. We drove to Ballarat to pick out my older sister's 21$^{st}$ birthday present whose party was that Saturday night. During the trip I got a little teary thinking about my mum and the deep sadness in her eyes from when I saw her that morning. I turned away and looked out the window so that no one would notice. It wasn't long until I was back at my mum's house. That afternoon when I returned there was a councillor there talking to my mum about grief and the kids, but luckily she was about to leave when I went to find my mum in the kitchen. I asked my mum what had happened and she told me it was an accident at work. I told her how I thought it may have been in the truck and she said it was at the Quarry where he worked. I asked my mum what actually happened and she told me that I didn't need to know, but for me it was important. I needed to know to process this and I think mum realised that. She told me what had happened and my heart sank. She told me not to tell the other kids as they would find out once they were older, should they ask. My little sister lost her dad exactly one week before her $7^{th}$ birthday. I felt so much pain for her and guilty again because I had known him much longer than they ever did and because I never treated him very well. Tristian was just 8 years old and had spent many long hours on weekends with his dad helping out when they went out to get wood to sell to make some extra money.

My step dad had a very strong work ethic and was always a very hard worker and that is something that Tristian has as a very strong trait from his dad, right to this very day. Garrett, on the other hand, was 11. He had been out several times to help with wood but wasn't much into the hard work of it all and was more interested in the truck shows and motor bikes that his dad would take him to see. I could see it from the moment I saw Garrett that he was broken. His heart was broken into a million pieces and this was going to be a very long journey for him emotionally.

I was astonished and overwhelmed at the amount of people that came walking through mum's front door that afternoon while I was on the couch in the lounge with the kids. Peter's friends just kept piling in one after another or several at a time to pass on their condolences. There were food platters sent from our local Safeway and IGA. My grandma was buzzing around trying to keep herself busy and make herself useful with us and anything else that needed to be done. She had spent parts of the day with mum and the kids trying to offer support but grandma's type of support isn't really of an emotional nature, rather physical…which was needed at that time just as much.

I remember my mum walking around lost for a long time. I saw her once up the very back of the yard pacing back and forth. I watched her thinking how lost she was, how much hurt she would be feeling and how angry she was. She had to be angry; I was angry. I had one constant sentence running through my head, "this can't be real, this kind of thing doesn't happen to my family, we're just ordinary people….this happens to other people." I was wrong.

Over the next few days there was people coming and going. I attended my sister's 21st birthday party and had a few too many drinks….this was a disaster on my part. I ended up going home to dads and going to bed with my misery in tow.

On the 4th of December my little sister was to turn 7, so mum decided to postpone the funeral until after her birthday, because she did need to enjoy a happy day with her friends. Grandma and I helped mum organise and throw a small party for Kal. I went down the street with grandma to one of the local shops to try and pick out an outfit of some sort for mum to wear to the funeral as she didn't feel like facing the public just yet. We were sent home with a few outfits for mum to choose from.

At that point in time I had blonde hair with bright pink streaks in it, and mum had asked me to dye my hair for the funeral, but me being me and as stubborn as I am, I said I wouldn't do because this is who I am! I really regret not having done that to this day. The day of the funeral came around and grandma was to ride with us in the car that the funeral director sent to collect us all. We arrived and were seated in the front row. People poured into the small chapel for well over ten minutes and I sat there like a stunned mullet staring at his coffin. The man who spent many many years putting up with me, raising me and working hard to be able to afford things for me was resting in there and all I could think about were those last words I said to him. I wished, more than anything, that I could take those words back or even better be able to say I'm sorry and ask for his forgiveness. I never got that chance and I felt that this guilt was what I deserved for being so callous towards someone who only wanted the best for me. As soon as the service started I knew I was going to cry a never ending river of tears, but when would they start? Within the very few first sentences of the service we were reminded that we were all present on that day to celebrate the life of Peter James Holiday, who died at the age of 42. The loving husband of Karen, father of Jessie, Garrett, Tristian and Chanel. It was at that very moment that I lost my self-control. I couldn't hold my pain or sorrow in any longer as I realised just how much he did mean to me, and I to him. He was no longer Peter or my step dad; he was my dad even if I already had one. The service was beautiful and, looking around at all the dismal faces in the crowd, I was amazed at how many people there were. Each pew was full to the brim and there was no more room left around the walls; there were people having to stand outside the door. My mum had "always" by Bon Jovi played for her husband and also "long way to the top" by ACDC who were his favourite band of all time. The service ended and the pall bearers took their places, each of them his good friends. They lifted his coffin to go on his final journey to where he would be put to rest. I wanted to stop them, I wanted to make them put him down; they couldn't take him away, he was needed, I needed him. I had to restrain myself from making a scene on a day that everyone would remember. We all rose and followed the coffin out to the hearse. On the way to the door I noticed Sally sitting with her Nan and pop and the tears streaming down her cheeks which made me lose my composure yet again. Just outside the doors I spotted my dad and sister who were there to offer support and for my dad to say his final goodbyes to a friend of his.

We drove to the cemetery; we were of course one of the first to arrive. My mum was so strong. I don't even think she realised just how strong she could be. She held herself together the best she could to give her husband the best goodbye, the one he deserved. I watched as the cars and motorbikes just kept coming and coming; there were so many people again. I couldn't believe so many people were there to say good bye to a much loved mate, co-worker and family member.

We walked to the spot where he was to be lowered into the ground. The dirt was covered with a fake green grass mat, and there were a few chairs for us to sit on so that we could be close to him. Darryl provided a basket of flowers for us to take one each and drop onto his casket as he was lowered. The final words were said and we were each offered a flower. We all got one except for Kal. She missed out. I think she was partially standing behind me, so Darryl didn't see her. She looked devastated but as Darryl was speaking again I didn't want to interrupt, so I gave her my flower. The flowers were all dropped onto his new bed, as he was being lowered into his final resting place. I felt a great relief in knowing that we were in the beginning of being able to take a step forward knowing he was at peace but uneasy about what was lying ahead. I have often felt that I didn't get to say my goodbye properly. I gave my final goodbye to my little sister because she missed out, but she deserved to have that final moment with him; he was her dad that she wouldn't have the privilege of getting to know for as long as I did.

Before we knew it we were thrown back into reality and there were few moments on the following days when I didn't think of dad or miss him. Christmas was around the corner. My mum was sad and I still couldn't help her. My siblings were zombies and someone was missing, someone we loved very much. We were to have our first Christmas without him. This one was going to be hard and I knew it and dreaded it. Mum persisted in keeping Christmas as normal as possible; she didn't want to ruin it and I think she appreciated the distraction the cooking provided. I was still living at my dad's and arrived at mum's in the afternoon to have tea with everyone. The food was great but all in all it was a miserable Christmas for everyone.

From the time we heard of the news of dad's death to the moment we were preparing to say good bye, I never really let anyone know how I felt. I needed to be strong for my family. I felt they needed me more than I needed them and that this was my moment to offer them support. I tried to remain positive although I was hurting inside and just as I did on the morning after hearing the news I shut off, which I did time and time again when my emotions would start to surface.

I threw myself back into my social life and school as I continued plodding along through life. Just a few weeks short of 6 months since dad's accident, I got home to dads from school and was told shortly after walking in the door that my pop had passed away early that morning. I was upset but I never had a great relationship with my grandfather. However, I was certainly overwhelmed with relief for both my pop and my Nan. For as long as I could remember he was in a wheelchair after losing his legs to ulcers caused by his diabetes. He was as deaf as a door knob and each time we went to visit, my Nan would always relay the conversation to him at the top of her lungs so that he would feel included. He always looked sickly and frail and his condition rapidly deteriorated in his final few months. On the morning of his passing, at around 10am he called my Nan into the bedroom and told her he loved her and then shut his eyes and peacefully went to sleep. I was relieved that he no longer had to suffer and could finally rest in peace. We attended his funeral which very few people attended as he had lost a lot of friends due to being so unwell. My Nan at the age of 60 had gone and got her driver's licence so that she could drive pop around to appointments because she loved her husband dearly and had devoted many years to looking after his health and well-being even at her own expense at times. My Nan had "amazing grace" played at his funeral which saddened me immensely. It brought back my memories and feelings of my nana George's funeral because the song had been played for her. That song holds a very special spot in my heart to this day and always will.

My mum ended up buying a caravan and I agreed to move back and live in there so that I would still have my privacy. I had started year 11 and life proved to be going back to normal. The more I shut off the more the pain faded, and that's what I needed in order to be strong and to move on. Over the next few years my mum was travelling to and from Melbourne occasionally for the court case regarding dad's death. Mum ended up with a court payout and we were able to live more comfortably. It never felt right and certainly not ever the greatest of circumstances to come into money. No amount of money can ever replace someone's life and just how precious that is, and this is why everyone should be more careful. While I am a very fatalistic person and believe that everything happens for a reason, this accident could've been avoided had the workplace complied with safe work practices and this was something I have felt very angry about with the boss and the company.

I turned 16 and got my learners permit. Mum bought me a car and life was great. I was growing up and becoming more and more independent and I loved it. Turning 18 was not too far away; it meant having my probationary licence and freedom was on the horizon. I just wanted to do what I wanted without anybody getting in my way, and that I knew would begin when I turned 18. My friend Anne from school had moved to Ballarat with her mum a year and a half earlier but we still made time to speak to each other and visit when we could. I completed school but with no career goals ahead, I had no final score to make up and only attended exams so that I could say that I had done them. Almost a year later I decided that I would move to Ballarat, to new experiences and an adventure. The idea was exciting.

Mel and I decided to move in together as she wanted to stay in Ballarat near her boyfriend Luke as her mum was moving back to our home town of Maryborough. We searched and inspected many properties but since neither of us was working, it proved very doubtful that we would ever get a house. On 27 September 2007, we were travelling on a main road in Ballarat when a car came out of an intersection in front of us. I had no time to react as they were too close. I screamed and remember seeing the lady's and children's faces just before impact. I screamed, the air bag ejected and the next thing I knew we were in the side street and bouncing gently off an incoming company car. Mel immediately fled the car; she had asthma and was struggling to breathe due to the powder from the airbag. I sat still, shocked, and looking at my bonnet that was now pointed as high as the roof of the car. A man appeared out of nowhere and did a quick check to see if we were ok before he called 000. Someone had reported the accident to the local newspaper whose reporter was there faster than the police and paramedics. I stayed in the car until I was examined and given the all clear. I called my mum and started crying. She wanted to come and get me but I told her to wait until the next day. My sister Mel who was just leaving Ballarat at the time was called by Mel to come back, and she did in a panic. My car was towed and as I almost passed out and fell back into an oncoming car, my sister felt it best to take me to the hospital which ironically was one measly block away.

I was in a neck brace and had x-rays. Mel was also in a neck brace and had an MRI done. I was given the all clear and took my niece with another friend Greg who lived in Ballarat with his girlfriend Ash to get some tea at Ash's place. Later on, Mel was discharged from the hospital. Her boyfriend at the time, Luke, was living at his mum's and they were both very quick to come to the scene followed by Mel's mum. We arrived back at Mel's mums flat after she left for work. As she worked night shift I would be sleeping in her bed, and being an early riser I would be up before she returned.

There were people pouring in left, right and centre and I couldn't handle it. I knew where the money came from that brought that car, the car I loved. Somehow we both managed to survive the car crash with very minimal injuries. I had a small bruise on my leg, and a rather sore neck. Mel, on the other hand, had a few more bruises than me. She had black and purple seat belt bruises, bruises on her knees from them going through the glove box on impact. She was quite sore as expected. I needed to do something and asked Luke's friend Josh, who I had taken a liking to, if I could go with him to play some pool to take my mind off things.

I contemplated the view that we survived with minimal injuries for a reason, and life surely now had to get better and quick. Many people looked at my car and commented on how the firewall saved both of us from being seriously injured. Someone was protecting us that day and it's because we still had so much to give, and so much to learn. I was looking at a more positive side of life and wanted to move on beyond the accident. It wasn't long before I had a job interview and we were approved for a house. My car was deemed a write off and I was to be paid out from the man's insurance company due to him being in the wrong.

Josh and I spoke often and after Mel and I got our house I was able to see him more. We moved in and all was going great I was independent and loved it. I had little money but I was determined to make it work. After just three weeks Mel decided to go and stay at her mum's with Luke (he had pretty much moved in with us). Mel was often good at over-dramatizing things and kept complaining about nightmares and anxiety from the accident. I didn't understand it, because I chose to move forward. I didn't need to be stuck in the past. I had a whole life ahead of me and it felt life was just beginning.

Even several months she had not come back but then told me one night she was coming to get her stuff on the weekend because she, Luke and two other people had a rental property. I couldn't believe it; I hadn't done anything wrong. I paid my rent, I paid the bills and I did the shopping but she was moving out. I just didn't get it. I was hurt and upset, but told her that I wished her well and reminded her that he name was still on the lease, so she needed to continue with her rent. I found out a few weeks later that she had not done that. She cancelled the direct debit and I was sent an eviction notice for overdue rent money. I didn't have $500 to make up the difference. I was so angry that I sent her a message and the response I got was that she didn't care if I was living in a cardboard box in the gutter. And I was horrified. I didn't know what to do and things were going well with josh and so it was him I confided in.

There was no way that I was going to have my name blacklisted when I had been paying my rent and had the bank statements to prove it. The real estate didn't care to contact Mel directly and because I was still in the house I had to deal with it. I applied for a small loan and was able to get just enough to cover the amount due, and decided to move out. I had found another place which was just around the corner from Sally's house. She moved in there with her boyfriend who also happened to be her step dad's younger brother. They had been in love with each other for years and resisted the urge for as long as they could. I found the situation odd but was happy for my best friend, and especially since they were expecting their first child.

Josh and I moved in together and times were very tough. I struggled with finding a job as I had limited skills, and had very low self-esteem due to this. Josh had to travel and stay in Geelong every few months as he was an apprentice spray painter and needed to attend trade school. I was often left with $40 for a fortnight after paying my share of rent and paying back the loan; luckily Josh paid for the groceries. I was at times left with very minimal food while he went off to trade school. The grocery money was needed for his petrol and accommodation. I began to think just how selfish he was but soon turned it around on myself because he needed the money so that he could keep his job after all.

Sally had a baby boy and I loved going around and spending so much time with them. When my niece was born I was 15 and I doted on her. Her dad was a dead beat and the decision he made to walk out of her life was probably the best decision he could've ever made on her behalf. I felt as though I owed it to her to be like a stand in "dad" I guess. My sister had become a single mum and struggled at times, so at the age of 16-17 I would volunteer my weekends to go and babysit so that my sister could enjoy a social life and feel normal. I was pleased to have spent so much time with my niece; she was beautiful and I have always thought of her as my own. I had thought many times about having kids of my own one day but that thought at that age scared me to death; I was just past nineteen. I had my whole life ahead of me with many things to do, yet I was still unsure of what they were.

I would often go around visiting Sally and Ryan through the day and enjoyed the happiness he brought me. I fell in love with the idea of becoming a mum and discussed this with Josh. We had both decided that we should wait for better financial condition, especially until he had at least finished his apprenticeship. I went on Implanon only to have complications and had to have it removed after a month and half. It was on 19 October just after our 12 month anniversary that I went to the doctors and took a pregnancy test. The results showed two lines and the doctor announced I was pregnant and congratulated me. I was stunned and asked him to repeat himself. The words echoed in my ears. I felt a glimmer of happiness but more fear than anything. What would I do? How would I tell Josh? I needed to tell my mum, but what would she say?

Josh arrived home not too long after I did. I sat him down and showed him the test and explained that the two lines meant that I was pregnant, that he was to be a dad. His reaction surprised me because as he handed me his phone to call who I needed he told me he loved me. That was all I needed at that moment because I was scared and didn't know what to do.

I was worried for a long time about having this baby, wondering if I would be able to look after a baby, how we would go financially, and whether I would be a good mum. I decided that this happened for a reason, and I was to take responsibility for my actions and raise this child who was yet to become one of the biggest parts of my life. My pregnancy was quite simple. At around 21 weeks I was taken to hospital and later found out that I had a 4mm gall stone. Quite a scary experience but also something that died down as quickly as it started. I reached my due date in no time and being 3 days overdue I attended my anti natal appointment. My blood pressure was up slightly and the midwife wanted me to stay for more obs. She decided to have extra tests done and scheduled me for an ultrasound the following week had I not already gone into labour. By sheer coincidence there was an ultra-sonographer on the maternity floor with all the necessary equipment and I was given a quick check. These words will never leave me: "your cords fine, your fluids fine but that's your baby's head in your ribs!" I didn't know what to do and after I was finished I sent my mum a message to call me. She was at school in Bendigo an hour and a half away and told me that they weren't to do anything to me until she was there. My mum has always been my rock, and I'm so grateful to have had her in my life. The decision came down to having a c-section that was yet to be booked depending on my blood test results. We left at 5pm after arriving for my appointment at 12:30. My sister spent the day with me and my niece who was only 4 at the time. She was so patient and well behaved and I was very proud of her.

We got just two blocks away from the hospital when they rang and asked me to go back in as soon as I could for surgery as I was already overdue. We got home, I told Josh what the plans were and he decided that he needed to have a shower and whatnot before he could come up. Besides him having two mates over at that time, I put it down to nerves. My sister and I went back to the hospital knowing that within a short period of time I would have my baby in my arms. In the meantime my mum was hurriedly heading to the hospital from Bendigo and wasn't going to miss a thing. She made it just in the nick of time really. Josh didn't want to come down for surgery as he has a weak stomach, so my mum came with me. I was so glad to have her there and that will always be a special moment for her and I. it wasn't long before I was numb and all was underway. I had my baby within 20 minutes! My mum brought him over to show me my son John. The first thing that came to my mind was the very minimal amount of hair he had and that was the first comment I made. I couldn't wait to hold him; he was finally here and boy, did he have a lot to teach me!

I couldn't believe just how much love you can have for such a small little person that you've only just met (officially). Once we were home and settled in, it didn't take long for John's lack of sleeping to take its toll. Mum stayed the first few days to help me out, and that was amazing. In a couple of weeks I was exhausted, healing from surgery and trying to keep up with the general housework. I was having a lot of trouble breast feeding and felt like a failure. My health nurse also contributed to this by being so pushy about it. Once I decided to put John on formula his sleeping improved and he started gaining weight rapidly. I felt amazing; life was good. He got his sleeping under control and was generally a happy and contented baby. It wasn't long before Josh and I started bickering again about his need to be with his friends all the time. I kept saying to him, "What about us?" but I truly believe he just took it for granted that we were always going to be there.

My dear nana Heather passed away when John was just four months old. I believe it was also due to a broken heart as pop died a few years earlier. I was unable to go and see her in the days before she passed due to lack of money and I have always been disappointed within myself for this. There was no way I was going to miss her final send off. I was mourning her passing but I tucked it deep down into the depth of my emotional holding pit and moved on with life.

Sally and I spent a lot of time together when the boys were young even after her, Phillip and Ryan moved to a new house. One night Josh, John and I went around for tea. Sally had her hand in Phillip' pocket and pulled out a small plastic zip lock bag with white powder. I knew exactly what it was. I knew he had a history but as far as Sally and I knew, that was finished. They had a fight and we left. She jokingly sent me a message later saying that he had left and would probably turn up to my house and no doubt proposition me for sex. I couldn't believe she would say that and reassured her that it was never going to happen. Within ten minutes of receiving that message my doorbell rang and it was Phillip. He had always made me feel uneasy and Josh knew this and was quick to come home when I told him Phillip was there. I went to bed and left the boys to their own devices. I later woke with a fright to find Phillip sitting on the side of the bed with his hand under the blanket rubbing the top of my thigh and telling me that we should go for it. I didn't want to panic. I didn't know what he would do, not to mention I was sleeping in bed next to my partner. I offered to go and have a smoke with him but that was all I was going to do. He asked again and I reminded him that I was best friends with his girlfriend, had a boyfriend and wasn't interested. I stood up and went back to bed. He left a while after that. I didn't know what to do and told Josh about it the next morning. He was quick to let both Phillip and Sally know what had happened and that he really wasn't happy about it. I was blamed by Sally and she took Phillip' side. I didn't expect much else but I certainly wasn't at fault. I lost my friend that day, the friend I had known since I was three, and I was very hurt.

Not long after John was born I had started speaking to Mel again. She had a six months old son of her own to Luke. I was made aware by a mutual friend of mine and Mel's that after the accident she sought legal action claiming compensation for the damages I caused her from a preventable accident. I was gutted and worn out. I couldn't have avoided that crash and the same evidence was obviously found through the solicitors as no case was ever made. I was becoming increasingly tired of Josh putting John and me on the back burner and was fast approaching my 21$^{st}$ birthday. I had planned a party and the night was a great success; I was well pleased with the festivities. My mum had John for the night, so we were both able to enjoy a night out together. It was almost as though a switch had flicked and I just didn't care about anything anymore. Something within me had changed. Luke was having the same issues with Mel at the time and we sought comfort with each other. We both knew what the other was going through and soon it turned into a short lived love affair. I broke up with Josh and Mel became suspicious of Luke and me. One night she confronted me through a text message. I confessed; I didn't want to lie as it never does any good. Luke, however, lied and told her I was making it up. I was so hurt and annoyed. Josh found out and I was devastated at the hurt I had caused so many people. This wasn't like me and I didn't know why I really did it. I like to help people, not hurt people. I was so ashamed with myself and this shame has followed me through my life ever since. I've always been open and honest about what happened with anyone and any abuse or comments that were made I wore because I deserved them; I needed to take responsibility for my actions and own my decisions no matter how bad they were. I ended up convincing Luke to come clean to Mel. She had a right to know and didn't deserve to be lied to, and I didn't think it was fair if I was being blamed and dealing with this matter while he was living it up as if nothing happened.

Our rental had been put on the market and it was time for John and me to move. It would be our first house together and things were looking promising. I was excited for our future. I was doing well with being a single mum, because all along I did everything myself anyway. I thrived on John's love and found something new to be proud of him for as each day passed. I was single and felt liberated; I could do what I wanted. The only downfall was that I became lonely at night so that I would have a few drinks to soothe myself. I had a son to look after and be a role model for and this was not acceptable. I stopped and made plans for both of us. I loved spending every minute with my son, and I felt he enjoyed his time with me. I later rented a computer and got pre-paid internet. I signed up with a dating site; plenty of fish.

I thought the internet dating scene was great. I was able to introduce myself to people and talk to them without ever having to get too close unless I wanted to. I could make it happen on my terms all the while having my son in my care, no baby sitters being necessary. I spoke to a few people on there but there was one in particular who caught my eye. In September 2009 I received an email from a man in his early 20's. He was looking to settle down finally with the hope of one day starting his own family. His name was James. I had found it hard before this man to find anyone who really wanted to settle down and who knew what they wanted. All I was looking for was someone who wanted to have a family, be a part of a family and love and respect my son and me. This was what we both deserved. We continued to talk through facebook for several months after that and went as far as having a few phone conversations. Things were going great and I was thrilled.

A few months prior to mine and James's first contact I allowed my best friend and her then 4 year old daughter to move in with John and me. My best friend

Natalie was having an extremely hard time and looking for a new start, so I offered them a place to stay temporarily so that she could get the ball rolling. It was great being able to have regular adult conversations again and we always enjoyed each other's company. As neither of us had millions of dollars we were often house-bound and spent a lot of time together. We were getting on each other's nerves. It wasn't long before other people were sticking their noses in and deliberately causing trouble between us.

On 9 January 2010, James rang me and with the generous offer from Natalie to babysit John I was to get on a train and head to Melbourne to meet James for the first time. There were a few hiccups on the way which resulted in James's mum coming to pick me up, and James thought that the night was going to end there. I have quite a sense of humour and prefer to make light of situations and I did that on this occasion. I'm glad I did because from the moment we met it was as if we had already known each other. We were comfortable and felt something instantly. It felt amazing.

James drove me all the way home to Ballarat and I invited him to stay, and stay he has done since. There have only been a few days during the period we've been together when we have been apart. He never left, and never wanted to. I didn't want him to. There was an amazing bond forming between James and John and I was falling in love quickly. Natalie got a house and moved in and I was happy for her but unfortunately the damage had been done and we lost contact.

After James and I had been together for 5 short months we learnt, on $2^{nd}$ June that I was pregnant. James had always wanted to be a dad and a good one. His dad was a stranger to him from such a young age and he never wanted to be anything like him. He resented him and didn't want to ever have his children feel that way towards himself. We shared out news with our families and everyone was over the moon. On the 3rd of June James got down on one knee and asked me to marry him. I was over the moon as I couldn't believe it. I was so happy; this was what I had always wanted – my own happy little family. I was excited for all that was ahead. My pregnancy was reasonably easy, with just a few little scares. Two weeks prior to my due date I started having contractions. I wanted to give birth naturally; after all I am a woman and it's what our bodies are designed to do. I had felt I had cheated with John's birth due to the circumstances and having to have a C-section. I didn't have to do the work myself; I didn't feel the pain or labour or giving birth. I felt it was an important experience for James who was becoming a dad for the first time and I was determined to deliver this baby myself.

We went to the hospital and were later sent home to wait and see if labour would be fully established. By morning I had no contractions and minimal sleep; I was tired. This continued for the next three nights. All the while I had John, who was two and a half, to look after during the day. I was uncomfortable and exhausted and wanted it to be over finally. On the Thursday night I was in more pain than I had been before the contractions were getting stronger slowly, so I decided to go to the toilet and have a shower. As I sat down on the toilet I heard a gush and felt a sense of relief that my water had broken. But when looked down I realised it was in fact blood. I became worried but didn't want to scare James, so I got in the shower. Then I called him and explained it to him gently and he called the hospital. The midwife wasn't very concerned, so we shrugged it off a little. The bleeding slowed but continued and James called again. We dropped John off and went to the hospital. I was admitted and put in a bed on a monitor. I finally fell asleep after James had climbed into the bed with me. I awoke early in the morning to a team of doctors. We had a discussion and they decided to do an exam. I was only 1cm with a slight sign of blood. The doctor decided to break my water to see if labour would progress. I was given 4 hours and then I would be having a c-section. My mum came over to be with us and James's mum drove all the way up from Melbourne to be there for support too. As the hours ticked away I didn't have any more contractions and was given another hour. I went for a walk and at the end of the final hour the contractions started. They were painful. I was exhausted and still had a small bleeding. I resigned to the thought of a natural birth and I was concerned for my baby's health and agreed to another c-section.

James came in with me and our mums waited upstairs for our return. Our son Angus was born and he was just gorgeous. It was love at first sight and I was ecstatic. I had a placental abruption which was the source of the bleeding and was able to take comfort in knowing that I made the right choice by undergoing surgery again. I was told that I was only going to be able to have C-sections from then on, although there was one hospital in Melbourne that allowed anyone to have a third baby naturally.

John loved being a big brother and wanted to smother Angus with affection. He was such a beautiful baby although I did struggle trying to manage my time with housework and ensuring that I gave them both extra attention. Although struggling at times with the concept of having a baby I was pretty relaxed because I had had a little practice. He worked nights and enjoyed being home and able to do the night feeds with Angus and having someone on one time with his son. When Angus was a few months old I started to feel really tired, and really down on myself. An accumulation of things from over the years. I did an online test via www.beyondblue.com and confirmed what I had thought. I went to my GP who asked me to complete a test for him which also confirmed I was suffering from depression. He prescribed anti-depressants which made me ill. I was annoyed at myself because I was so down in the dumps. I woke one morning with almost an epiphany. I don't need pills to make me feel better! I CAN make me feel better. I had taken the pills for three days and returned to my doctor informing him of my decision on which he commended me. I started looking for part time work and came across an advertisement for a short course for certificate 3 in home and community care and aged care. I applied and was accepted. It was three days a week and I really enjoyed it.

Not long after the course started John was admitted to hospital to have a small procedure done. He was having a lymph node in his neck removed for a biopsy. I had the process started when I was around 28 weeks pregnant with Angus. I researched on the computer the reasons for multiple enlarged lymph nodes in the neck area. I had asked two doctors about it previously but both gave different answers. There were many different reasons for this to happen and the worst were leukemia, Hodgkin's disease and non-Hodgkin's disease. I took John to a new doctor and explained my findings. I was scared for my son; I felt guilty for what was about to be done to him but I didn't want him to suffer either. I wanted to know if there was something wrong with him so that we could hopefully fix it, and the whole time I dreaded the thought of hearing that heart shattering news. John underwent several tests and needed the biopsy. I went to theatre with him and held him while he went to sleep. I couldn't help it; I burst into tears. I didn't want to leave him, I didn't want him to be scared if he woke up with strangers, and I had to wait upstairs. His dad was at the hospital waiting with James and me after he came out of surgery. Very sleepy but glad to see us all.

The results revealed that John was clear of any serious diseases and his malady was narrowed down to just having hyperactive lymph nodes and what a relief that was! I was so happy that my baby was healthy and thriving and didn't have to suffer. It was a massive weight lifted off my shoulders and I felt a new light around us all. Although there were no treatments required it felt as though he had overcome an illness and we had a whole new positive lease on life.

I continued with my studies and did exceedingly well. We had three weeks of placement mid-course and just at the start my gall stone issue decided to rear its ugly head. I would be in agony for 6 hours at a time, and often wouldn't get to sleep until 4 or 5 am and be up early to continue my placements. I plodded along and made sure I continued because this was something for me, something I could use to help support my family too.

I had a phone call from James early one morning whilst I was at school. He asked me to come home because we needed to go to Melbourne; his pa had suffered a stroke. James loved his Pa dearly. He was like his dad and his best friend. I knew this was going to be a hard time for James and that he would struggle, and I wondered if I would be able to support him in the way he needed. We drove to Melbourne and waited with James's family until Pa was taken to the ICU after surgery. Only two people were allowed in at one time and Nan sent me in with James's cousin Anne. I felt terrible because I was going in before James, who was going in with his sister Ellen. I should've waited; I should've gone last. We walked into the room and up to pa's bed where he lay still with tubes coming out of his mouth and machines all around him. I was taken aback and couldn't believe the condition that this beautiful man was in after having seen him the weekend before sitting at home in his chair drinking a cup of tea. The doctors came and spoke to us and explained the extent of his injuries suffered from the stroke. My eyes filled with tears for James, his family and for my sons. I felt terrible pain and sadness for what was taken away from such a beautiful soul but couldn't let my emotions get in the way. I offered James my support with a gentle hug and we headed back out. I was scared for James to go in, scared of his reaction; this was going to cut him up so deeply. He absolutely adored this man and I wondered how he would cope. The next time we went to visit he was awake and just before we left for home I went in to see him by myself. I asked him how he was. He looked at me with sad eyes. I nodded and said I know. "Pa, I know I've never said this; I wanted to thank you for welcoming John and me into your family and I want you to know how very much you mean to everyone including me." He grabbed my hand as if to thank me. I kissed him good bye and told him I would see him again soon.

We all knew it was a matter of time; so we all made so much effort to spend as much time with Pa as we could. It was clear soon that Pa could still recognise everyone and the look on his face when he saw baby Angus, whom he cherished so much, will never be forgotten. We celebrated an early father's day and everyone gathered in Pa's new private room. I had a basic surgery the day before and was sore and uncomfortable but there was no way I was going to miss this opportunity. There was so much love and joy in that one room for one person, one person who was so special that he touched everyone in a very unique way. It broke my heart to see many people I cared about hurting but everyone soldiered on to make the most of their time left with Pa. I would often well up on our trips home thinking of Pa and James's struggles at that time and that was my only release. I needed to be able to support my soon to be husband when he needed it and I couldn't do that if I was a blubbering mess.

I was still having trouble with my gall stone and had minimal sleep most nights. James decided to stay at the hospital one night with his uncle James to keep Pa Company. Over the previous few days pa was becoming increasingly tired and we knew that time was running out. At around 1:40 am on 19 August James's phone started ringing, I knew exactly why. It was a relief to know that he went peacefully with his wife by his side. He was so strong and hung on giving everyone time to process what was happening and what was yet to come. He fought and fought and made everyone proud, and finally he could rest. I knew it was a long road ahead especially for James. I would often walk into a room and find him crying quietly, but I was pleased to know that he was letting it out. I knew the funeral would be especially hard. James, Ellen and their mum Lauren stood in front of everyone, reading their eulogies; each was very proud of the man they loved and now mourned. They spoke of stories from when they were younger and James spoke of his best friend, his Pa. I was proud of them all, and extremely proud of James. He was strong, brave and composed himself to deliver his eulogy the best he could for a man that deserved the best.... And he came through!

Just before I finished my course I had been playing with the thought of relocating to Melton for a while and one morning woke up and felt the pull to do it. I spoke to James about it and within two weeks of making a decision we had a rental property and were soon moving. I looked forward to what was ahead. I had plans to start work in aged care as I had completed my studies. There were more job opportunities in Melton and suburbs close by. It was going to be an adventure. I also decided that since James had lived in Ballarat for almost two years away from his family and friends, it was my turn to compromise.

I had another surgery a short five weeks after my previous one to remove my gall bladder; finally the pain and sleepless nights were coming to an end. I was so glad to finally have it over with. I was asked by my surgeon to stop taking my birth control pill two weeks prior to reduce any complications. The morning we got the keys for our new house I thought I was late, so I took a home pregnancy test and it showed a positive result and I was excited. Perhaps my body was still adjusting I thought. Not even a week after moving I decided to take another on the Sunday morning and much to my shock the test was positive. I thought I was going to have a heart attack. I wasn't ready for this, Angus was only 9 months old and I felt I would be taking away from him, not to mention John who had an ever increasing attitude.

James took the news quite well, as did most people. I was in shock for quite a while about it and feared having the struggle adjusting to three children as I had at times with two in the early stages. Troubled times came and went frequently. James was depressed and still grieving the loss of his Pa. I was exhausted and ran down and bore the brunt of James letting out his emotions. It was a time where both of us were unsure if we were going to make it to our wedding that was planned for the 9th of November 2012. I would wake in the mornings and wonder if today was going to be a good or bad day, whether James would have another outburst and if I was going to be able to handle it. I held my head high and continued on. I was strong enough to deal with this; I was his rock and he needed me. Although he hurt me time after time I stayed; what kind of person would I be if I walked out on him when he needed me? I loved him with all my heart and hoped that he would find the strength to seek professional help. I was flooded with relief when he finally decided to speak to someone. I could see a light at the end of the tunnel and I was proud of him. He took control of the situation and even joined a local gym and life was becoming a constantly happy place again.

Growing closer and closer to my due date again I had numerous midwife appointments as my measurements were smaller than they should be. I lived close enough to be able to go to the hospital that would allow a natural delivery after two c-sections and that's what I planned to do. Unfortunately I was advised that our baby wasn't growing very well and agreed for the safety of my baby to undergo another surgery. Our daughter Willow was delivered on the 2nd of July and we were so proud. She was beautiful. She weighed 5 pound 11, small and very delicate. She was perfect. When we got home she was such a peaceful baby; she wasn't very needy and was happy to wake, eat and then sleep. She is our healer. She helped heal our family and even though she wasn't planned, she was very much needed. Both her brothers love her very much and smother her with affection regularly.

Just before my birthday while I was around 26 weeks pregnant I was told that my great grandmother had become very ill and was probably only going to have a few weeks left. I had decided to go and see her that Sunday but on Friday night I received a phone call off mum with the news I dreaded hearing. I missed out on saying goodbye; I missed out again. I was devastated and angry but also relieved for my great grandmother. She passed at the ripe old age of 92 and lived in her own home. My grandmother was her sole carer and helped maintain her health as she was diagnosed with dementia a few years earlier. I hadn't seen my great grandmother since her 90th birthday because I was afraid to visit. She didn't recognise any of her family other than her two children. It would've broken my heart for her to not know who I was, so I took comfort in the time we had already had together.

James and I got married on 9 November with the love and support of our families. We had a fantastic day and were very happy. Our children were all present to see our union and I was pleased with how far we had come. It was a beautiful ceremony and the night was filled with lots of love and laughter. James and I had lost family members that were very dear to us but knew they would be around to celebrate with us. After the wedding I didn't know what to do with myself. I had put so much time and energy into planning everything that I didn't have anything for me. I was at a shopping centre with James one afternoon and felt compelled to go into one of the shops I had never entered before. Within a moment I had a pack of tarot cards in my hand and was heading out the door. When I was a teenager I used to read tarot but never had a great grasp on the idea of reading, how to do it and why; it was more like a "game" if you will. I decided to study the cards and learn to read them the best I could and see what guidance and wisdom I could attain. I started a journal as suggested for studying each of the cards and realised a lot about myself. Since then my sister in law and I have opened an online business doing readings and offering people guidance. We don't have qualification and certificates saying that we are certified to do such things, but what we do has is personal experience. We don't need to force ourselves upon anyone; we can simply offer some "wise" words.

While writing my journal I discovered that there were certain tarot cards that appeared threatening to me. These were actually hidden fears and negative experiences I've had, and through recognizing this I was able to deal, assess and put this behind me. I have over the years gathered a set of rules for myself to live by. I have learnt from my past mistakes and don't want to relive them. I don't want to hurt people, but I want people to know that they don't have a right to hurt me either. Sometimes things aren't dealt with in the right way and upon reflection I can understand this and make a mental note to try a different approach in the future. I'm certainly no saint, but I know how I would feel in certain circumstances and I don't want to be guilty of making anyone else feel those emotions.

This year I am making a point to accept help from others if they offer. I'm not bulletproof and although I always try my hardest I can't do everything and I'm learning that it's ok to accept help from others, just as it's so readily accepted from me. I don't consider myself a very outgoing person; I think of myself as an observer in new situations. I tend to sit back and watch how people interact with one another and this is a very helpful tool I have found. In saying that I seem shy and reserved which I am at times but you can bet your bottom dollar that I'm sitting back and taking everything in. I feel calm, I feel relaxed and I don't feel so stressed. I've let go of my overwhelming need to clean my house all the time and accept that just because I'm not up and about doesn't mean I'm not doing anything. I can now allow myself time to sit and read, or play on the floor with my children....why because they chose ME, me of all people to come as a parent in the physical world. They did that for a reason, so I need to be as positive and reassuring for them as possible, even if their characteristics are poles apart and they do drive me batty..... that's why I love them.

I have found a lot of comfort in spirituality and had sought out different mediums to have a connection with my dad. I had for over a year been reading many books by psychics and mediums and all the things they were saying made so much sense to me. I wanted, I needed, to know more. I'm a firm believer in life after death and after searching for a medium I felt comfortable with, I finally had a reading. It was a thought I had dabbled with for a while but based on my own assumptions I thought it would cost a fortune and I would be hard pressed to find someone who could do it. How wrong I was! I was able to validate that it was in fact my dad coming through and was able to ask and receive genuine answers to my questions I had waited so long to ask. That night after the reading I processed the information and when I woke in the morning I felt like a new me. I was positive I was happy and satisfied. I had confirmation that he forgave me and still loved me just as he always did. I can be at peace in knowing that he is often around which he proved by mentioning a few recent incidents that this lady would never have known. I don't know if calling it the path to enlightenment is appropriate but I'm looking up from here on and going to improve the person I am and the person I become.

I have proven to myself time and time again that I am strong and I can move forward, and I believe that this also comes from my mum. She is such a strong woman and has put a tremendous amount of effort into raising her four children with very minimal help. We've all grown up with respect for others, to be polite and knowing since we were young that we can achieve anything that we wanted so long as we put our minds to it. My mum has often been my rock especially when it comes to being a mum myself. Raising three children is far from a walk in the park but the love they give me and the love I have for them is priceless, and I never want to miss a thing.

I used to hold onto and harbour all of my emotions. I'm practicing positive affirmations daily, and changing many things about myself for the better. I now try to talk about my emotions with others, so I am not holding them in to explode. I can reflect back on my life and see the valuable learning curves along the way for me. I've learnt that sometimes friends aren't forever. They're around to stay or they've come into your life to teach you lessons and help you grow. Just the same as hardships. I believe that we can learn from good and bad but I also feel very strongly that bad times are necessary for positive personal growth. If I have a hard time now, I ask myself before bed, "What is it that I am supposed to learn here?" "How can I benefit"? These are things that you should ask. Ask for good fortune and abundance for yourself. Each and every person on this earth has a right to thrive and experience life's greatest pleasures. We all have a journey, we all have a story to tell and no one should be judging another until they've walked a mile in their shoes. Life isn't about being down, it's about being the best you can be, the happiest you can be and making the most of what you have; only then will you know true happiness, the new found love.

## About Jess Welsh

Jess Welsh is a psychic medium who has just completed her diploma in life coaching. While having been through tests and trials herself, Jess understands the importance of empowering individuals and providing them with the tools they need to live their best life. Life is a journey, it's not meant to be suffered.

## Soul Sistas Healing

Check out this popular online community on facebook

Website www.soulsistashealing.com

## White Light Publishing House

www.whitelightpublishingau.com

# Embracing the Dream

## Written by Karen Mc Dermott

I have always been a person who followed my heart. This has often gotten me into bother and even though I have always had the most sincere intentions of not knocking anyone over on my way towards achieving my dreams I have on occasion bumped into people on my journey.

I look back on my 37 years thus far and WOW is all that I can say. I have been very blessed in many ways. I did go through a dark period in my early 30's but I was fortunate enough to have been enlightened as a consequence of it and so I am grateful for the insights into my depths that I have received because I am now a more complete and wholesome person for experiencing them. I will not go into detail about my journey to enlightenment as I wrote about that in detail in *Journey to Inner Light* that has already been published and some readers of *Living a Positive Life* may have already read it.

Wisdom is something that I have come to value immensely. Simplicity is underrated in my view and we as human beings make life way more complicated than it needs to be. I have discovered that our first reaction to things is often an emotional one and that the head comes in to create balance at a later stage and it is then that we should react. I watched an interview that Oprah had with an Irish Author who wrote a book filled with this type of observations. It made sense when he said that with a confrontation it takes more to step back and let it pass by. Detach yourself from the situation immediately. This can often be perceived by the naive as an act of cowardly behaviour but in my experience it takes more courage to take that step back and any regrets that I have in my life come from not taking that step back as the consequence of the alternative can send ripples throughout someone's life, altering it without even thinking!

I suppose having children has focused my attention elsewhere. I am now a mum to 5 children and I don't want them making the mistakes that I made but I decided early on not to dwell on that. I choose to parent with love and it has served me well so far. Don't get me wrong; I am no angel and I have yelped a few times but my focus is to parent through love and when my children have something that they need to learn I guide them firmly with love through that issue. I don't like instilling fear into them as I feel that doing that harms their emotional wellbeing and only shows them how to instil fear in others and let's be honest, the world does not need many more people with that mentality.

I have embraced wholeheartedly the principle of the Law of Attraction and although there are many things that affect my life that I don't control I know that I can control how I react to them and I am always conscious about thinking about everything as positively as I can. Making the best out of every given situation is something I have inherited from my mum; she is a very resilient

Living a Positive Life

woman who always does her best to pursue a positive outcome even in the most negative of situations.

That is why her latest challenge is her biggest test of all. I am living at the other side of the world and sometimes feel useless in her dealing with her challenge. I know that by remaining positive and being that someone she can ring anytime, I am doing a little bit. I am also only a plane ride away and I am very grateful that the world is not as hugely limiting as it once was.

As conscious as I am of the miraculous things that are possible through fully focusing on what viberations you are sending out, there it is tremendously hard to control the feelings connected to someone you love being sick. This is when I allow myself to honour them, have a huge cry and call in my friends for support; then when the surge of emotion pass I find that I am more clear of mind to make decisions. In the past I would have bottled it up but that is not helping anyone. By releasing and taking positive action I am instigating the best possible outcome.

I am very lucky that I live a positive life, I am grateful for it and because of this I know that I will continue to live a positive life because life is often about perspective. If you believe in the positive then positive will find you.

I am able to stay at home with my children and that is a really wonderful thing for me. Because of this I have been able to write books and pursue an interest in publishing books also. I now own Serenity Press Publishing and even though we are a small publishing press now I know that it can be as big or small as I want it to become. I am amazed at how far we have progressed in such a short period of time that is totally by believing that anything is possible, not setting limitations and embracing opportunities as they arise. I am able to help authors bring their dream of becoming a published author to life in a positive way and that is a wonderful thing.

On a more personal note, my third novel is about to go to print. I have seven journals published and I have also created Mamma Macs Home-made Children's books. These are books that I created with and for my children which we have decided to publish and in doing so we are raising money for a children's charity because they were created through love and wonderful things need to come out of their publication. I will write more about writing and my journey in our next collection *Writing the Dream*.

I try my best to be true to myself while still being the type of mum, wife, daughter, sister and friend that I can be given my circumstances. We all have choices and our choices determine our life. I have created the life that I have by doing what I feel is best in every situation and following my heart when I can. I don't embrace everything as the timing is not right when some things present themselves but I always like to remember a quote that always sticks with me, "What is for you will never pass you." If you want to experience something and the timing is not right, it will come back to you at a later stage.

I have written many articles along my journey that can be viewed at www.buildingbeautifulbonds.com that I hope are useful to *Living a Positive Life* readers so if you have a moment why not grab a cuppa and check them out.

I think that the best advice I can share with anyone is to be true to you. If you really want something, pursue it; those who love you will support you if you want it enough, and be patient because then you will enjoy the process of achieving your dreams as it is important to savour our beautiful lives.

## About Karen Mc Dermott

Hello, I am a wife and a mum to 5 wonderful children; this is what I am most proud of. This is closely followed by my passion for writing and desire to make the world a better place.

I am also the proud founder of Serenity Press Publishing. It is a publishing company with heart that just keeps growing. I thoroughly enjoy compiling collections of inspiring stories and helping first time authors get published in a positive way.

I am an author of three spiritual based romance novels *The Visitor, The Wish Giver* and *The Memory Taker*.

Through the love of teaching my children new things I created *Mamma Macs Home-made Children's Books*. This is how I first began expressing my creativity in 2008 and now I am sharing these books with the world to hopefully make a positive difference.

In 2010 I discovered the Law of Attraction and it fascinated me beyond belief. I can now very easily manifest in my life and I do this through love. I am now an Advanced Law of Attraction practitioner and actively helping others manifest their hearts desire.

I am truly blessed. ☺

# Serenity Press

www.serenitypress.org

Check us out on facebook

Mamma Macs Home-made Children's Books

www.mammamacs.com

Check us out on facebook

Various Authors

# Free Bonus mini book for you to enjoy

Book 1 of the 'All it takes is an Hour' Series

by Rod Willner

onLiving a Positive Life

# "All it takes is an hour"
# Awareness and Contentment

### Written by Rod Willner

## Introduction

Hi! I hope you're comfortable wherever you are. Got a cuppa? This should only take about an hour, so let's begin.

Firstly, I would like to say that if you are reading this little book of mine, thank you for picking it up and I really do hope that you enjoy it. Secondly, I would like to give you some of my reasons for writing this.

I believe that we should look for wisdom from many different sources and take what we need from each one and discard what we don't. No one book or piece of advice can possibly tell us exactly what we need to know for the rest of our lives. We are constantly growing and forever changing, so the words of wisdom that we seek should continue to inspire us throughout our lives. Also we are all very different as individuals. There are no two people alike in this big world of ours, so wisdom should also differ for each person.

There are many self-help books available today. I have read a lot of them and have learned a lot and I would encourage you to try them yourself. There are some great reads around! That said, I haven't written this book to try to place myself in the same league as some of these writers but to hopefully add a little of my own.

Lastly I would like to say that I have learned a lot while writing this little book. I would also like to thank all the forces that were involved in putting this together. So let's go!

I'm going to get straight to the point and tell you only what you need to know, understand and put into practice, the meaning of two simple words, in order to be happy in your life.

The first word … **Contentment.**

This is a very powerful and simple word with an all-encompassing meaning. So what does it mean to be content? And what am I content with? There are easy answers for these types of questions, so let's take a look.

The good thing about contentment is that it is a feeling, or emotion, that can be felt across all aspects of your life. Contentment can be coupled to relationships, family and friends, finance, career and lifestyle. Literally, anything you do, love, enjoy, experience, etc. Understanding its meaning unveils a powerful tool for building happiness. To know the word and to understand it is easy, but to put it into practice, well, that's a little bit harder. But the rewards are fulfilling and lifelong, and the best part is that you get to control every single aspect of it!

So, how can we be content? Well, it's time to look inward and ask some serious questions, and provide some honest answers.

Take a look at all aspects of your life and paint a mental picture of the things that you are not content with, be it a relationship, where you live, your looks, your career, etc. If it helps, write it all down. Now ask yourself, why you are not content in these areas. What is it that makes you feel this way?

When thinking about things that we're not content with, there's often something else that creeps into our thoughts… and that's comparison. We compare ourselves to just about everything and everyone. Why do we do this? Well, the answer is that it gives us perspective. But is it a good way to get perspective? Should we avoid comparison altogether? No, definitely not, but we should change the way we compare. This is what I believe to be the best way of turning discontentment into contentment. Let's explore this.

Some would advise to avoid comparison at all costs and that it is a destroyer of dreams. "You are one and you are unique," they say. "You are not the same as anyone else on this planet." "Who you are and what you do is truly original." Although these words are true, this is not necessarily the best advice. A different approach is needed.

When we hear people say "never compare," they are usually referring to comparing with people that are better looking, are more successful, have more money, better relationships, etc. And by doing this, we inevitability feel worse off. But, what if we were to compare ourselves to someone that is less fortunate, someone that does not have money, good relationships, etc.? If we did that, would it not paint a better picture of ourselves? Would we not have more appreciation for what we already have?

One of my favourite sayings has always been "compared to what". A comparison can either be a very positive experience, or a very negative one, depending on what we actually compare to! So, compare all you like, but be content with what you have, and work on what you have. Because there is always someone worse off than you! Ok, let's keep moving. Don't let your cuppa get cold!

The next word ... **Awareness**

I think the phenomenon of awareness is more powerful than anything else. In fact, I could have written this book entirely on awareness alone!

So what is awareness, and why is it so important? Awareness is your key. It is what unlocks your feelings and your emotions and sets you free. It has the power to give you a good day, or a bad one, a happy life, or a sad one. Awareness is all encompassing, and we have to understand this to be able to use it to our advantage.

There are different things that we should be aware of, and these things provide different advantages for us. For example, if we focus on being aware of ourselves, our own feelings and emotions, we will, in time, begin to understand ourselves better, which in turn will give us a better quality of life. That's a no-brainer right? Isn't that what every self-help guru talks about? But wait. There's more! What about the awareness about others? How does that affect us?

When we become aware of others, we notice that the things we say and the things that we do (our actions) have an impact on others. We can then quickly and easily work out what provides a positive reaction, and also what provides a negative one.

We can then adjust how we speak and act around others in order to bring about more pleasant interactions with those around us. This is like changing the future, or influencing destiny, because you can literally change your day, your week, even your life, by being aware of how your words and actions affect others. And more importantly, how it affects you. It really is that easy!

A few years ago I put this to the test with a young man that I used to manage. He agreed to partake in an experiment with me, and it went something like this. Every day for a week, we were to go out for lunch and look around the shops. We would interact with as many people as we possibly could, in the cafes, shops and even in the street.

It was agreed that I would do what I normally do. Smile at everyone I interact with, speak nicely, ask how his or her day is, get to know as many of the shopkeepers on a first name basis that I could and generally create a nice vibe between myself and the people that I interacted with.

My employee, on the other hand, had completely different instructions to follow. I asked him to speak directly to the people that he interacted with, only asking for what he wanted or needed, never smiling or saying thank you, hello or goodbye. Basically, he was to remain stoic and unemotional. He did this (very well I might add) the entire week during our experiment.

The following Monday we went to lunch to talk about what we had experienced the previous week. For me, it was a good week full of nice experiences. I met lots of new people, and knew most of them by name, and they knew mine. They remembered my favourite coffee and what I liked for lunch. I even got a free slice of cake! They smiled at me and said hello each day. To sum it up, my week was quite a pleasurable experience.

My friend, on the other hand, had something completely different to report. He didn't have a good week at all! He had received bad service from people. Some of them had stopped smiling at him and spoke to him quite abruptly. One young lady in a café even tried to ignore him and not serve him. In summary, he was not really happy about his experiences during the week.

So it's pretty obvious to see what went on here. I created a happy environment for myself using no more effort than he, just by treating others differently and being aware of how my words and actions influenced those people. He only achieved feelings of being miserable, and probably influenced those he interacted with to feel something similar.

He never believed that he could influence his future, his state of mind and his happiness, let alone influence others. He does now!

Be aware of what you say and do. Understand how your actions and words affect others. It's just like cause and effect, action and reaction, or you can call it Karma if you're more comfortable with that term. It's not that hard; in fact it's really simple… if you try.

## Putting it all together.

This is where the fun stuff begins. It is also where things get a little difficult. But as I mentioned earlier, the rewards are lifelong.

**Awareness and contentment…** we all know these words, and we understand them. But how do these two things connect? How do we couple awareness with contentment? The answer to this is actually quite easy… Be aware of what makes you content! Make it your mantra, your positive affirmation!

I am aware of what makes me content

I am aware of what makes me content

I am aware of what makes me content

This statement might seem too simple, and you'd be right in thinking so. But if put into practice it can become the key for you to find happiness. Have a think about this. Put this book down for 5 minutes. Better still, go and make another cuppa!

Back again ... got your cuppa? Good, let's continue.

All you have to do is become aware of the things that make you feel content. The things you say, your actions, others around you, your relationships, your career, your friends, your children, your location, your age, your looks, etc. Being aware of what makes you content can put all of these things into perspective.

Put contentment into your thoughts. Contemplate it as often as you can during the course of your day. Focus on it, and focus on everything that you have in your life that brings you contentment and ultimately makes you happy.

This should become a state of mind, a kind of conditioning that will bring upon happiness. And remember that what I'm talking about here is a change of thought, a shift in thinking, so to speak. This does not require any additional effort. Just a change in the way you look at things.

Pretty soon, this awareness will start to change the way you act, what you say, and even the decisions you make. You'll begin to understand the connection between your words and actions, and of the effects on others and of this phenomenon.

Over time, this will become automatic. It will occur without you even thinking about it. Sure, you'll stop and notice it occasionally, but ultimately this will happen without you knowing it, and without effort. It will continue to go back and forth until you find a balance that does nothing but sustain your happy state of mind.

You'll be walking around with a silly grin on your face, perplexing those that fix their eyes upon your expression. Making them wonder just what you've been up to, to be smiling like that. Oh, and wouldn't they like to know!

You'll feel a constant bliss and complete contentment (there's that word again). You'll radiate nothing but confidence. Your family and friends will notice a change and people will ask what you've done, or what you are doing to be so happy. You'll start to feel more alive than you ever have before. You'll be more confident, empowering and strong. Your relationships will grow stronger and deeper. You'll make better decisions, achieve more, and ultimately be more successful.

All of this can, and will, happen. But it is not something that is going to happen quickly. It took me a few years to get to the point where my awareness drives almost everything that I do. I was a bit slow on the uptake. However, you may grasp this concept and put it into practise very quickly, and then begin to notice the changes. However long it takes for you to get this working, just trust that it will be worth it; I can personally vouch for this.

## Dealing with negativity...

How do we deal with negativity and negative people? It's an unfortunate reality that some people like to put others down when they are trying to improve themselves or better themselves. It is also inevitable that you will act kindly and speak nicely to some that may not reciprocate.

It is important to note that not everyone that you smile at, speak nicely to and treat kindly is going to react in a positive way. Let's face it; some people seem to prefer to just be grumpy all day! However, this is about you and the changes that you can make to enrich your life, so focus on the people that react kindly. As for the grumpy people… just smile at them more; it makes them even grumpier. But hey, don't tell them I said that!

As far as other people's opinions are concerned, the most important thing that I can tell you is this. Don't worry about what people say or think! Just like that old saying, "What people think of YOU is none of YOUR business." It's easy to say but hard to do, right? Indeed, but remember that this is your life. This is your trip; it's your ride. You (yes you!) get the final say in everything concerning you. It's only a choice, and it's a choice that you can make starting today!

## Conclusion

It is my wholehearted wish that you can take something from this little book of mine and use it to help you be a happier person. If you already are a happy person, perhaps you can help a family member or friend to be happier in their life. Just as the movie says, "Pay it forward".

So that's the end of our short time together. I do hope that our exchange has been beneficial. Exchange you say? Yes, writing this little book has been a learning experience for me too.

As I leave you now, I have just one thought in my mind … I wonder what we can talk about next time?

You ponder that, and I'll put the kettle on.


## More to come in the 'All it takes is an hour series'

'All it takes is an hour' ~ What is our purpose?

'All it takes is an hour' ~ Is it ok to be alone?

'All it takes is an hour' ~ Dealing with negativity

'All it takes is an hour' ~ Why am not happy at work?

'All it takes is an hour' ~ My relationship sucks!

'All it takes is an hour' ~ What is religion?

'All it takes is an hour' ~ Take it all in

## About Rod Willner

Rod's love of words began at the age of 13, when he started writing poetry. At around the same age, he also discovered a passion for music. It wasn't long before the inevitable happened and these poems began to turn into songs.

His passion for words (and music) is still strong as it was when he began to write, and remains an integral part of his life. Helping to heal, helping to grow and helping to love.

Rod now lives in Chiang Mai, in the North of Thailand with his wife of 8 years and 3-year-old son.

# Thank You

A huge Thank You to everyone who has taken part in this book.

It takes courage beyond belief to open your heart and share your story and I am positive that there will be many people who will be grateful that you cared enough to share your journey.

We at Serenity Press are very proud of the team effort that brought this book together.

Our wishes are that our contributing authors continue to experience a positive life and that our readers treasure the positives in theirs.

Wonderful Wishes,

Karen, Serenity Press